HAUNTED NORMAN OKLAHOMA

JEFF PROVINE

Haunted America

Published by Haunted America
A Division of The History Press
Charleston, SC 29403
www.historypress.net

Copyright © 2014 by Jeff Provine
All rights reserved

First published 2014

Manufactured in the United States

ISBN 978.1.62619.563.9

Library of Congress CIP data applied for.

To Bob & Debbie

CONTENTS

CONTENTS

PREFACE

Ghost stories became a regular part of my life when the OU Ghost Tour began in the 2009 Halloween season. I was working in the English Department at the university then, recently returned from a backpacking trip in the UK. Having studied abroad there some years before, I ventured back to check things off my to-see list and visit old friends. I toured everything from Inverness, Scotland, in the north to the Isle of Wight off the south coast of England. During that summer, I attended ghost tours in London, Edinburgh, York and everywhere else I could find one. There was no shortage, either; with the land having been settled for more than one thousand years, there seemed to be ghosts anywhere someone started to look.

In my own experience, I knew of only two ghost stories. One was an old family legend about the "Baby Ghost" in our home. I grew up in the house my great-great-grandfather built in 1894, on land he had won in the Cherokee Strip Land Run the previous year. My parents returned to the house in 1976, remodeling it and having four sons there, in addition to my sister, who had already come while my father finished medical school at Baylor in Houston. According to family lore, when there was a baby in the house, my parents would awaken in the night to the mournful sounds of crying. They would pull themselves out of bed to go check the baby's crib and find him sleeping peacefully as the crying died away. This happened again and again, but only while babies were in the house. When one brother grew to sleep through the night, the cries would stop. When the next baby came along, the wails started up again, only to fade away as he grew up, too.

The story that began the OU Ghost Tour was the ghost boy of Ellison Hall, the first student infirmary on campus. Campus legend says that a boy was roller-skating on Elm Avenue next to school grounds. Some versions of the story say that he was hit by a car, others that he had an asthma attack, but both agree that he was in desperate need of help. He was rushed into Ellison, the nearest medical facility, where he died in surgery. The boy's spirit is believed to still roam the building, now offices for the College of Arts & Sciences. He bounces a ball, plays with gurneys, rides the elevator from floor to floor and causes motion sensor lights to flick on when no mortal is around. People claim to have heard his giggles and even blame him for messes in their offices.

When I related the roller-skating boy's tale to Tess on the Isle of Wight, she suggested I make a tour for the school. I doubted there were enough stories, but once I began researching the buildings on the century-old campus, I discovered all kinds of hidden history and strange happenings. It turned out to be enough for a whole collection, which became *Campus Ghosts of Norman, Oklahoma*. As of 2013, more than three thousand people have taken the OU Ghost Tour, and many of them stopped by afterward to ask about spooky stories in Norman.

Once again, I didn't know many stories at all. But as soon as I started looking, the stories made themselves known. The city is packed with tales of bygone citizens still walking the earth, making stairs and floorboards creak, raising hairs on the living and sometimes even appearing as otherwise unexplainable sights. Beyond the ghosts, Norman carries stories of gangsters, lake monsters and a gold rush. If anyone considers history boring, they aren't taking a good enough look.

Even more important than the stories is the history of our community. People might know Norman for its connection to the university or as a commuter suburb for Oklahoma City, but our city is so much more with a vibrant art scene, some of the best eats in the state and bustling festivals. No wonder people stick around even after they die.

ACKNOWLEDGEMENTS

Special thanks go out to all those who helped in the research for this book by offering their time for interviews and leads on where to look. I would like to thank Erin Smith and Sue Schrems at the Cleveland County Historical Society; Joseph and Nancy Stine at the Timberlake Rose Rock Museum; Kim Lock, Dee Downer and the crew at Kendall's; the staff of Griffin Memorial Hospital; the rangers at Lake Thunderbird State Park; the hardworking team at the Sooner Theater; the easygoing fellas at Midway Barbershop and all the folks at S&J Antiques, Johnnie's, Hollywood Theaters and S&B Burger. Thanks to all of the facilities management staff, secretaries, public relations liaisons and faculty at the University of Oklahoma and Norman Public Schools who took time out of their busy schedules for interviews. Thanks also to Rick Smith and the National Weather Service. Christy Clark and the team at OKPRI gave great lessons in research and parapsychology, as well as applying science and historical evidence from Kathryn Wickham to the ghost investigation. Special thanks to Joe Griffith, Sally Austin, Lara Kelly, Bob Oliphant and Charles Burnell for sharing their own stories.

And thanks to everyone who stopped me after a ghost tour and said, "Do I have a story for you!"

Introduction

The ground on which Norman, Oklahoma, rests today goes back to time immemorial. Geologists tell of an Oklahoma from millennia ago that rested along the Western Inland Seaway. The hills to the east served as the shore to a landmass called Appalachia, where Cretaceous dinosaurs roamed. Meanwhile, the sea carved out flatlands to the west that would make the iconic, rolling Great Plains. As the land aged, the North American continent rose, and the water drained away to leave rich grasslands. Herds of bison millions strong roamed these plains and, after the introduction of horses, served as the main source of food for Native Americans.

The land that would become Norman stood at the eastern frontier of the realm controlled by Comanche, known as some of the most skilled warriors in the Southwest. Osage tribes lived to the east before their removal to northern Oklahoma, and for centuries the two battled back and forth over the rich hunting grounds. In his book on the history of Norman, written as part of the celebration for the U.S. bicentennial, John Womack describes Osage braves hunting Comanche scalps, as well as buffalo, to prove their masculinity. There is no clear evidence of Native Americans living for an extended period in the area, but many Normanites believe certain areas of the town were once used as burial grounds. Through its thousands of years of history, there is no doubt that some people would have been buried where today roads, malls and houses stand.

Water is as important as land when it comes to attracting human settlement. As French trappers and traders voyaged up into the Louisiana Territory, they found rich harvests between the Little River in the north and the Canadian River to the south. Hunters could find beaver pelts among the trees that grew up along the water or travel out into the plains for buffalo hides. The first Americans into the area were United States Dragoons, under Major Stephen H. Long, attempting to map the rivers of the Plains. In August 1820, the men struggled through the heat, blowflies and seed ticks along the path that would one day be Highway 77 between Norman and Noble. The famous writer Washington Irving, known for *The Legend of Sleepy Hollow*, accompanied United States Rangers from Fort Gibson on a reconnaissance mission in 1832. In what are today Moore and northwest Norman, Irving and several of the rangers spent an exciting day hunting buffalo to serve as provisions for the long journey home. They spent Halloween night alongside a creek feeding into the Little River, just north of where Lake Thunderbird stands today.

Overhunting slaughtered the bison, whose meat was largely wasted as hunters sought their hides and bones instead. Hungry mouths back east called for Texas beef, but the lack of industrialization in the South meant that ranchers had to drive herds across Indian and Oklahoma Territories. Jesse Chisholm, who had long served as a guide and interpreter, organized a trail through the Unassigned Lands at the edge of the Citizen Potawatomie and Absentee Shawnee lands. It was one of many cattle trails that brought herds up to the stockyards in Kansas along rail lines and eventually joined up with the main Texas Abilene Trail that ran along the path of U.S. Route 81 today. Chisholm's Arbuckle trail (which often becomes the name of the whole western trail) started at his trading posts farther east and followed a path perceived as dangerous from Indian raiding parties and outlaws. It was west of the Shawnee Trail in the more stabilized lands of the Five Civilized Tribes. Chisholm sought to fill the gap, as did men seeking profit like the Blue brothers, who established a trading post atop a hill, which is now Southeast Forty-eighth Avenue beyond Highway 9.

Railroads built into Texas eventually ended the cattle trails, but the Unassigned Lands were hardly quiet. Bands of would-be pioneers saw the ground as good for farming and attempted to force them open for settlement. These boomers (a name that is still heard cried out in Norman) eventually won political support, although the federal government had long anticipated their interest. In 1870, the U.S. Land Office contracted engineers to survey the whole of the Oklahoma Territory. Among the surveyors hired was twenty-year-old Abner E. Norman, who unwittingly granted the town his name.

Norman was born in Normandy, Kentucky, in 1850. Upon leaving school, he journeyed west with his classmates in search of surveying work. A wagon

Norman's Santa Fe Railroad Depot.

brought them to Fort Arbuckle, where they were hired under the federal contract. Norman first served as chainman for the survey area but was quickly promoted to leader of his party. According to a letter written by his grandson J.C. Norman in 1974 to John Womack, physical strength was very important to the leadership position. Without any other form of social enforcement on the open Plains, the head of the troop had to be sure to get work done by any means necessary. A strongly built man despite being so young, Norman was promoted because of "his ability to lick anybody in the gang."

While surveying in 1872, the party made camp at what was nicknamed "Indian Springs," a colloquial term used throughout the West for an unclaimed spring. This spring stood south of what is now the intersection of Classen Boulevard and East Lindsey Street and fed into Bishop Creek, which still runs through the middle of Norman's south end. The campsite is believed to have been used often before Norman and his crew arrived with their surveying equipment. As one of the few places in the area to receive regular water, a grove of trees stood up from the tall grasses of the prairie. French, Indian and American hunters would have stayed under the cool canopy, drinking fresh spring water between expeditions for buffalo, deer and bear.

The surveyors set up their own camp on the lonely prairie while they patiently marked the nearby border of the Unassigned Lands with the reservations for the Citizen Pottawattamie and Absentee Shawnee. As a joke one night, the men scraped the bark off an elm tree and took hot irons from the fire to scorch the words "Norman's Camp" in their young leader's honor. The joke must have been in good humor since he was able to beat them all up.

Norman's Camp stuck as a name. The next year, Montford T. Johnson, a Chickasaw rancher who was tired of seeing wolves harass his cattle, sent his foreman and a crew of African American hands to build a dugout there. During the next two decades, the artificial cave would be home to scouts hunting wolves and watching the cattle drives to ensure Johnson's cattle weren't rustled along with the others.

A new surveying crew arrived in 1886 to prepare for the coming of the Santa Fe Railroad. They moved into the dugout at Norman's Camp and decided to mark that name on their maps. The next year, when the rails came through, it was officially Norman Depot, although the only ones who lived there were the families of railroad agent Andrew Kingkade and foreman J.L. Hefley. The Hefleys were an enterprising lot and set up a boardinghouse for railroad workers. Since the railroad right of way was the only place trains stopped between Purcell and what would become Oklahoma City, they sold biscuits and coffee at whatever price they saw fit. On the night after the Land Run, when food supplies had run low and folks who had lost out on finding a claim were looking for something to eat before heading back to the Chickasaw Nation, biscuits went for six for a dollar (over four dollars apiece in 2014 money). Hefley himself made a claim downtown and set up the first Hotel Norman. His claim was later revoked since he was in the territory before the cannon signal, albeit legally as an employee of the railroad.

The Hefleys were the first of many interesting characters who would populate Norman over the coming century. In the 1930s, the "Einstein of the Mob," Murray Humphreys, moved to Little Axe, just east of Norman. Western film actor James Garner was born in the back of a grocery store in the tiny community of Denver Corner, where Lake Thunderbird now rests, and struggled there through the Great Depression before venturing out to Hollywood. In 1983, the Coyne brothers and Michael Ivins started up a rock group in town called the Flaming Lips.

Many of Norman's most story-worthy individuals were attached to the university, which has always been a driving force for the town. Many can remember the "Glove Man," who often took it upon himself to direct traffic while wearing heavy black leather gloves. He would also have arguments with telephone poles about his mother. "Three-Hat" Willie wore his three hats and liked to play tricks by shining flashlights at drivers as they passed or sneaking up on people with a bicycle horn. Michael Wright practically

Students returning to Norman in August. *Courtesy Cleveland County Historical Society.*

lived at the Bizzell Memorial Library, doing research to prove his conspiracy theories about the CIA, AIDS, OU president David Boren and noisy dogs in certain neighborhoods.

Perhaps the most infamous couple in town was Jim and Wendy Berlowitz. Jim earned his PhD in chemistry and then returned to school for a doctorate in Chinese philosophy. In the meantime, he taught himself to play the guitar. When he saw a truck knock over a parking meter, he took it home and installed it on his porch, charging people nickels to hang out. The Norman Police Department, which had been after Jim from time to time for his various herbal antics, arrested him for grand theft auto and stealing public property related to parking control. Jim defended himself in court and made no contest to having the meter, but he requested that the city prove that it was in fact city property. According to town legend, the case was thrown out due to the city not having proof. Jim returned the meter, and he was allowed to keep the nickels inside.

While Jim was well known around town, his wife, Wendy, became nationally famous. Toward the end of the spring semester in 1972, she was teaching English composition and decided to put her belief that "everyone should have the right to take their clothes off" into action. She performed a naked poetry reading and was subsequently fired for indecency. Wendy attempted to get her last paycheck through the courts and eventually gave up as the university began asking for some of her students to sign complaints for public exposure, which would have gotten her arrested. She then called for the law to be changed in all fifty states and made a "topless tour" of protests that included the White House. The attendees at her rallies were what Jim called "15,000 dirty old men," and Wendy became frustrated that "all they want me to do is take my blouse off…They don't want me to talk; they don't want to hear what I have to say."

According to Wendy, Jim was killed by bandits in Mexico in 1984. The couple had been moving around for several years, living as street musicians in San Francisco and starting up a mail-order record collection business with secret vaults in Dallas. The two were camping across the border in their station wagon, seeking out a house where Jim could spend more time writing his novels, when they were attacked, and Jim was shot three times. Wendy managed to escape, and she told her story to the Dallas newspaper.

As fascinating as Norman's living characters are, stories often turn to talk about those who return from the grave to haunt the town. Cemeteries, both continuing and forgotten, dot the landscape and give a feeling of not being alone. Old buildings where thousands of feet have passed still echo with sensations of persons coming back from the beyond to visit. Residents are often so attached to their homes that not even death can make them leave it all behind. Even the creeks, rivers and lake are said to be haunted by both ghosts of the long departed and creatures for which science has no explanation.

Whether benevolent, nasty or simply strange, Norman has a town spirit that is rarely quiet.

I
DOWNTOWN

In preparation for the Land Run of 1889, surveyors marked out quarter-mile sections that a lucky runner would be able to claim for his or her own. In addition to the large country sections meant to become farms, townsites were laid out with smaller sections that would become businesses and neighborhoods. On April 21, 1889, the town consisted of empty prairie, with a railroad track running through it and wooden stakes poking up through the sod. On the night of April 22, Norman already had 150 people camping under the stars after an exhausting day racing from the border. On the day of the run, many of the townsfolk rode the train from Purcell, which had exploded to ten times its size in the weeks leading up to it. By the 1900 census, Norman had grown to 2,225 people and hosted the University of Oklahoma, with its campus carved out of Charles Gorton's cornfield.

The pioneer spirit was practically a fever in early Norman. Prior to the run, a group of railroad men, businessmen, publishers and civic leaders created the loosely legal Norman Townsite Company. The plan was masterminded by Delbert L. Larsh, who picked men with certain key skills from those he knew were thinking of settling the area. Gorton and Pryor Adkins were ranchers who knew the townsite thoroughly from running cattle and cutting hay on the land. John Helvie was a locomotive engineer for Santa Fe who also knew the land and, more importantly, knew the engineer who would be driving the northbound train on the day of the run. The others included those with the appropriate public relations and capital resources to start the town. The men all signed an agreement outlining an ethical guideline, which detailed certain obligations and restrictions of future Normanites. It placed rules on the cleanliness of privies, required the burial of dead animals outside of town and forbade breeding horses in public. No known copy of the agreement exists today.

Most of the men made the run on their claims by riding the noon train from Purcell. To ensure fairness, no one who would be staking a claim could be inside the territory before noon on April 22. Soldiers were placed at the river crossings and along the border to keep out "sooners," who wished to sneak in to grab choice land. After the run, it became known that Purcell's noon northbound train had arrived in Guthrie at about 12:12 p.m. Those aboard, including Delbert Larsh, were adamant that the train had not crossed into the territory early. In fact, the entire train had been stopped at the Canadian River by soldiers who were waiting for the starting signal. The eager settlers waited in anguish during what Larsh described in 1939 as "the longest ten minutes I ever spent in my life." Finally, the cannon sounded, and they were able to stake their claims. The train, meanwhile, apparently made the rest of its sixty-mile run at over three hundred miles per hour to be in Guthrie a few minutes later.

Even if the men did cross early (which is likely, as it has since been proven that Guthrie, Edmond, Oklahoma City and most other major townsites were largely scooped up by sooners), they were shocked to find tents and campfires already set up around the railroad tracks. The Santa Fe Railroad had made huge investments in switches, sidings and station grounds, and it sent in members of its surveying crews whose work was now done to claim

Downtown Norman shortly after the Land Run of 1889. *Courtesy Cleveland County Historical Society.*

the land. As they were employees of the railroad, they were legally able to enter the territory, but they were subsequently fired, which made them eligible for claims. The surveyors filed their claims at the Guthrie Land Office, and the land was later sold to the railroad.

Although Larsh's initial plan for the town had been pocketed by the railroad, the Norman Townsite Company began to build up a new community. Larsh set up a furniture store. Adkins established the Planters Hotel. Ed Ingle, publisher of the *Purcell Register*, started a newspaper for the town called the *Norman Transcript*. When B.F. Smith attempted to claim the entire west side of the city in 1889, the company came together to prevent it and elected a formal town council from atop a lumber wagon. Other businessmen, plumbers and doctors soon moved in, and within a few months Norman was blossoming. The town did not grow as quickly as sites such as Kingfisher and Guthrie, and the outlying communities, nicknamed "Corners," survived for decades to come before being outpaced.

One such community, Franklin, continues to serve as a neighborhood with Baptist and Methodist churches, nestled in the countryside nine miles northeast of Norman. In 1895 and '96, Franklin hosted the area's famous gold rush. As part of the final settlement for land grants to claims, the homesteader had to sign that there were no precious metals or minerals known on the land, which would make it an industrial operation rather than a farm, as the land was intended. Rumors ran wild that homesteaders who came across veins of gold would keep them quiet until signing their last papers and then "suddenly" find a rich strike, making it all theirs without the legal restraints on homesteads.

These rumors turned into a rash of gold fever. People began to say they had come across evidence linked to gold veins, and soon meetings were held in the local schoolhouses to drum up money for stock in mining operations. When money wasn't available, people could sell their services through work at the dig sites for one dollar a day, paid in stock. Important men such as Professor Edwin C. DeBarr, then the young chemistry professor at the university—one of four faculty—and the *Transcript*'s editor, Ed Ingle, helped spread the word. Territorial governor and president of the Norman State Bank, William Cary Renfrow, denounced claims of measurable gold anywhere in the region.

The explanation for why gold had not been found was that it was hidden in the black rock deep below the surface. As miners kept trying, they found only more and more brown sandstone. Not even iron pyrite, fool's gold, was readily discovered. Ultimately, the cause was lost, especially after a Shawnee newspaper pointed out that the expense of transporting ore to smelters

Busy Norman trade near the train station. *Courtesy Cleveland County Historical Society.*

would make it cost over sixteen dollars per ton to mine, while the best ton of gold ore yielded at most fourteen dollars. One excavation managed to dig thirty feet deep before finally giving up.

About the same time in Denver Corner, Dr. S.O. Chesney was given a madstone in lieu of payment by one of his patients. A madstone is a stone removed from the stomach of an herbivore, a type of bezoar used specifically to "draw out" poison from a bite or sting. In the 1890s, rabies was a particular problem on the prairie, and the principal method of defense was to cauterize the bite with red-hot iron before the disease spread. If the hydrophobia continued, medical advice recommended soaking a madstone in hot milk and pressing it so it would stick to the wound. When it no longer stuck, the patient was supposedly healed. Chesney was something of an entrepreneur, running a cotton gin for a time, and the madstone seemed to be a good investment. It was rented at five dollars per week, and patients often lined up for a chance with the stone in the summertime. Eventually, the Pasteur vaccine for rabies was introduced to the territory, and use of the madstone dropped off. Evidence is vague about whether the madstone worked, but in a time when there were few other options, five dollars per week did not sound unreasonable.

While there were multitudinous schemes to get rich quick in early Norman, most of the real wealth centered on its bustling downtown. The first cash crops of cotton rolled in during the 1890s, and farmers spent the money at stores that grew up around the train depot, which had to be rebuilt over and over to be large enough to suit the town. W.H. Seawell established an opera house at 109 East Main (Mr. Robert's Fine Furniture today), which became the first three-story building in town and the cultural center that hosted the first community Christmas. There, Normanite William Renfrow had his reception after being appointed territorial governor by President Cleveland. To this day, downtown is a lively center with parades, the annual Music Festival and Second Friday art walks.

In its twelve-decade history, downtown has collected shadows in its corners. Past residents are said to still roam the buildings, either as guests of hotels past or workers still at their jobs, not knowing they have long been dead.

THE WHITE LADY

Sooner Theater

The Sooner Theater is one of the most iconic buildings in Norman. It stands with a sense of reawakened majesty, with its old-style colored-glass windows and gold- and yellow-brick façade. From its position on the corner of Main Street and Jones Avenue, beside the railroad tracks that served as the lifeblood of the town until the interstate came through, it was one of the main attractions for folks pulling into Norman's station on the southward trip from Oklahoma City. At night, the big vanity bulbs cast a brilliant ochre glow that lit up the west end of Main Street. To this day, an image of the outstanding green sign, with its gold letters proudly spelling out "Sooner," is visually synonymous with the city of Norman.

The first building on the site was the two-story Planters Hotel, established by Pryor Adkins in May 1889. He rushed to complete construction as soon as possible to foster the growing number of visitors to the newborn town. Salesmen were particularly interested in the new market, visiting with shopkeepers who could peddle their wares or even traveling out to farms to make direct sales calls for farming implements and household improvements. More and more immigrants came to the town, buying claims from homesteaders who decided to sell out or divide what they had into smaller, more profitable lots.

The Planters Hotel was the first brick building in Norman, built with material from the brickyard in Noble, seven miles south along the railroad.

The Planters Hotel once stood where the Sooner Theater is now. *Courtesy Cleveland County Historical Society.*

Adkins most likely chose the name to appeal to the Southern variety of farmers who were populating the area. With the first harvest of cotton that fall, Norman practically seemed part of Dixie. Late-harvesting crops like wheat did poorly in the early years due to drought, but it was not long before the weather changed and cotton was outpaced by agriculture more suited to the Plains.

C.M. West, the first dentist in Norman, rented out a room on the second floor on a long lease in late 1889 to establish a more permanent office for his practice. He had previously come to town only periodically and rented a room in Norman's second hotel, the St. James, which was said to be a crudely constructed building, little more than a frontier bunkhouse. The Hefleys, who had long dominated the hotelier business in the area at their home, later built the Hotel Norman, which won back a good portion of the market.

The Sooner Theater, as it has stood for nearly ninety years.

By 1929, modern tastes had outpaced the rustic comforts of the Planters Hotel. The building was torn down and replaced by a new brick structure designed by Harold Gimeno. Gimeno was the son of Patricio Gimeno, a Peruvian artist who had spent his life studying in Spain before being invited to the University of Oklahoma as a professor of art in 1911. Patricio headed the Art Department and later came to head the Department of Romantic Languages (with his native Spanish), while painting portraits for wealthy clients throughout the town. Harold carried on his father's artistic reputation as an architect, designing several houses in Norman before being contracted to create a theater.

The result was the Spanish Colonial–style building—popular in the 1920s—that stands today. The project operated under a $200,000 ($2.7 million today) budget that provided for imported mosaics and Italian marble. Patricio Gimeno was brought in to hand paint the 252 Spanish coats of arms that adorn the ceiling of the theater. A lounge for ladies on the mezzanine was laid out to accommodate those who might need to take a break from the boisterous productions, and a hidden soundproofed cry room for babies was tucked under the balcony in the back. When the project was completed, Gimeno went on to his next: the Spanish Renaissance gray-stone Beta Theta Pi house on Chautauqua Avenue, east of the university campus.

The theater would become the sooner, a term that had changed meaning dramatically over the years. In the days of the Land Run, a sooner was a cheat who had come into the territory sooner than was allowed by the sound

of the starting cannon. By the time of statehood, a sooner was a progressive who thought liberally while maintaining a sense of ethics, looking for new and better ways of doing things. The Sooner Theater lived up to its name, placing numerous advertisements in the paper as having "refrigerated air," "cooled water fountains" and the brand-new technology of audio synchronization to film—"talkies."

For years, the Sooner was the new cultural center for Norman. Patrons would pay ten cents for children and a quarter for adults to watch the last days of vaudeville and the Golden Age of Hollywood on the screen. Many teenagers had their rites of passage being employed as ushers or popcorn girls. In 1945, a movie was stopped to announce the end of World War II. During the film *Lawrence of Arabia* in 1962, the concession stand was told to add extra salt to the popcorn, to go along with the scenes of the desert and drum up extra demand for soft drinks. Just before intermission, an employee dropped the enormous drum of Coca-Cola syrup, creating a tidal wave of sticky sludge. As workers struggled around the mess, alternately trying to clean it and serve customers, the film let out a horde of thirsty moviegoers. The scene nearly turned into a riot.

By the 1970s, the Sooner had been outpaced by larger multiplexes and was barely scrounging an audience for B-rate movies. At last, in 1975, the theater gave its final showing, *Attack of the Amazons*, and closed its doors. A fire broke out later on, damaging the building and rendering it unsuitable for anything without major renovation. The City of Norman bought the building for demolition.

Concerned Normanites joined together to form a nonprofit to save the theater and rented it from the city. Donations poured in from citizens with fond memories, and the Sooner was returned to its former glory. Today, the theater has over fifteen thousand attendees each year at

The ghostly White Lady is said to descend the stairs.

concerts and stage play productions. The Sooner Theater, Inc., hosts community performances, as well as kids' camps in its nearby studio, once the University Theater.

Along with the rebirth of the Sooner, many believe a spirit from the past has come to wander the halls of Norman's "Grand Dame." Called the White Lady, she is most often seen alighting the east stairs, walking with grace and poise, unaware of those around her. The lady is described as a woman of indiscriminate age and striking beauty. Those who see her say she seems to glow with white light. She wears jewelry and a shimmering ball gown.

Others say they have seen her on the balcony. While the lady on the stairs is composed—practically emotionless in her elegance—on the balcony she seems to be in some kind of trouble. She appears in corners, or sometimes walking slowly down the hallway, at both times staring off at nothing at all. Those who have attempted to approach her are met with nothing but a fading vision or turn a corner and find her gone completely. People claim to have heard the sounds of crying, both the sobs of a woman and the soft, high-pitched wails of a baby.

Nancy Coggins, who serves as development director for the Sooner Theater, says that in her years working there, she has never seen a ghost. Despite all of her evenings helping out with performances, daytimes in the office and being up all hours of the night—even to dawn—working on grant proposals, she has yet to see any evidence of activity that couldn't be explained by the building's age. Even if there had been a ghost, she must have moved on.

Others still hold that the White Lady continues to haunt the theater. No one claims to know with certainty whom the woman might be. There are those who point to the theater's glamorous past, claiming that she may be a fallen starlet from the last days of vaudeville, bemoaning the coming of movies. Different witnesses say that her clothes are much older than the theater's golden days in the Depression, when people were eager for any piece of opulence, even on the screen. Instead, they say she must be from the days of the Planters Hotel, an unknown guest who met a tragic fate. If a woman wearing such a luxurious dress were a hotel guest, some record of her death would surely have been kept—even whispered about if covered up.

Whatever her story might be, it hangs as a mystery in local legend.

CUTTHROAT RAZOR

Midway Barber Shop

An old joke goes, "There are two jobs that'll always be around: barbers and undertakers. And you only use an undertaker once."

Soon after its founding, Norman's first undertaking business began in the furniture store of Delbart Larsh and Thomas Waggoner, members of the Norman Townsite Company. The coffins, both simple wooden boxes and ornate caskets, were considered the last furniture anyone would need. Barbers, meanwhile, were for the living, and a few gradually established businesses as the population of the town grew.

In 1893, the Davis brothers, Sherman and Otho, moved off the farm their family had settled in 1889 and set up a barbershop in town. Rufus Sherman Davis, born in 1869, was the elder brother and guiding force behind the venture. The younger Otho Eugene Davis, born in 1881, was full of energy and bright ideas on how to bring in loyal customers. Their advertisements fill the pages of the *Transcript* in the 1890s, taking up three different slots of the local news on April 17, 1896, to remind readers again and again that "the Davis Brothers will treat you right. Give them a call," their "shop is the place to go for a neat hair cut or quick shave" and that they should "Try Davis Brothers, the barbers."

The brothers did well but had stiff competition from other shops that sprang up around town. A stroke of luck for the brothers (and misfortune for a quarter of Norman's downtown) came in 1902, when a whole block of the south side of Main Street burned, including the competing Wheeler's Barbershop. The block was quickly rebuilt as Norman continued to grow. Meanwhile, the brothers continued to find new ventures, such as Sherman selling pedigree horses from Kansas.

As barbers, the two were the center of town gossip and always ready to follow through on a new opportunity. In 1907, after two unsuccessful bids, Sherman won the office of county treasurer. He was elected on the Democratic ticket, which was a difficult position to gain as politics within the party routinely shifted others away from donating bonds toward his campaign. Once he was on the ticket, he did well, being narrowly defeated in his first run before winning the first of two consecutive terms in 1907. In 1916, he was back in office again, running on a platform of local experience. He said, "I am one of the pioneers of Oklahoma and every dollar I have made has been spent here and I have paid taxes every year since I moved

The Midway Barber Shop.

to Oklahoma." While running, and while in office, Sherman kept up his barbershop business.

Sherman made political gains, but local legend holds that Otho became increasingly troubled. His wedding announcement to Willie Ventress in 1902 calls him one of the best young businessmen in town, but his endeavors later turned little profit. Matters grew worse in 1916, when their son C.L.

died at age two. Otho ended up living in the apartment above the brothers' barbershop with his wife and five surviving children.

The story goes that, in 1923, Otho was at work giving a man a haircut before his shave with the long-bladed straight razor for which expert barbers are famous. The blade is kept sharp by being beaten at an angle against a leather strop, which forces any imperfections in the metal in line rather than simply removing them like a whetstone. For each classic shave, the barber freshly strops the razor. The result is an incredibly sharp blade that requires a skillful hand to guide the angle and a careful eye to check for bumps in the skin.

Lately, times had been very tough on Otho. He had lost a good deal of money, and having so many mouths to feed made it difficult to collect enough capital for any new ventures to regain his fortune. He had joined the Odd Fellows and, according to storytellers after the fact, a few secret societies that had strange religion. Those networks had proven useless and were even drains on him. Working as hard as possible in the barbershop seemed to be the only way to stay afloat. There didn't seem to be any future beyond that.

The telephone rang. It was Willie, calling from their apartment above to see if Otho had a moment between customers. He hadn't started on the shave yet, so he told her to come on down. Willie went down the rear stairs from the apartment and slipped in through the back. There, she told her husband that she was pregnant once again.

Otho reportedly didn't have much of a reaction. Willie went back upstairs to the children, and he went back to his customer, finishing the haircut. His hands went through the expert motions, practiced a thousand times. When the haircut was finished, Otho wrapped the man's face in a steam towel to soak his whiskers for the shave.

While the steam set, Otho stropped his razor. He quietly excused himself and went into the small bathroom at the back of the shop. The razor was in his hand.

For a while, no one noticed Otho's absence. Finally, the customer in his chair pulled off the steam towel, now gone cold, and asked about Otho. Another barber, presumably his brother Sherman, went to check on him.

They found Otho on the floor, his throat cut open with the straight razor.

Despite the loss of his partner and brother, Sherman kept up the barbering business until his retirement, when he sold the shop. Though the barbershop has changed locations, owners and even names over the years, it claims to

The upstairs apartment, untouched for decades.

carry the same spirit. With more than a century in downtown Norman, it is one of the strongest competitors for oldest businesses in town.

Today, customers still get haircuts and straight-razor shaves at the classic shop. It has been updated over the years, collecting memorabilia to decorate the walls. It is floored with charming black-and-white tile, and mirrors line the walls to show all angles of the barbers' handiwork. A handsome barber pole, with red and white stripes, hangs outside. The atmosphere is quaint, welcoming to conversations on any and every topic. Listeners can pick up countless stories of local oral history, which will most likely never be recorded, from Midway barbers Steve and Mike.

Many of the stories focus on the shop itself and its ghost barber. The barbers working there routinely suffer from objects disappearing from their shelves. Combs, guards for the electric clippers and chair clips seem to walk away of their own accord. Everyone teases one another about being thieves and pranksters, but they feel confident that no mortal is mishandling their equipment. The barbers have stories of time and again struggling to find their clip guards, searching high and low for them even for weeks on end and finally coming across them out in the open, where they know they have looked

Items sometimes leap from the shelves or disappear for weeks on end.

before. These always seem to be very light objects, never heavy shears or the like, as if whatever is moving them does not have much earthly strength.

More eerie, and with less explanation, are the spontaneous movements from inanimate objects. Cabinet doors, kept shut with spring locks or magnets, sometimes spring open. Other times, they open slowly, almost imperceptibly.

Decorations set up on shelves fall off as well. Skeptics might speak up about micro-earthquakes or minute vibrations that cause the baseball caps and bottles to eventually waddle their way off. That might explain some objects that sit for years, with no one touching them, and then fall. More curious are the ones that sit well back from the edge and then suddenly leap into the air of their own accord.

Away from the swiveling chairs, the back of the barbershop has its own strange happenings. There, a table once held a popcorn popper; it sat next to the door that leads into the supply area and restroom in the rear. From time to time, people would notice that it seemed to slide away from the door. No one thought much of it, dismissing the table's movement to the building being old and maybe having a cockeyed floor. One morning, as the crew came in to open the shop, the table had staggered out into the middle of the floor, blocking off the doorway, despite no one having been there that night.

Nighttime also brings strange occurrences while no one living is in the shop. The barbers lock up in the early evening and rarely come back later on, usually only to grab something forgotten before heading back out again. Yet even though he knew that all of the lights were shut off when he locked up, Steve has driven by on a number of occasions and seen them back on.

Others have seen the lights, too, at all times of night. Often they will claim to have seen the light at two or five o'clock in the morning. When the barbers come in the next morning, the lights will be shut off again.

One customer said he saw more than lights. As he drove by in the early morning, the lights were on. Slowing down to peek inside as he passed, he saw a shadow standing over one of the chairs, looking just like someone cutting hair. The next morning, he asked who was getting his haircut at such an awful hour, but no living soul had been there that night.

Steve says he has time and again felt a sudden cold draft in the shop, particularly while in the back waiting for customers. Even though he was alone, he would get chills and the feeling that he was "not the only one in the room." His co-worker Mike said that he had just "gotten used to it."

The barbers agree that, if there really is a barber ghost in the shop, he should stop spooking around and help out with the work.

DARLIN'S

Denco's Café

As Norman grew, much of the east remained residential areas leading toward the campus for the Central State Hospital. Its downtown, meanwhile, spread to new businesses toward the west, particularly when the naval base was established in World War II and later on as I-35 was built. Some of the first institutions west of the railroad tracks were restaurants, trying to be the first place hungry customers would see as they came into Norman.

Today, sitting on the southwest corner past the railroad tracks, is S&B Burger Joint, a recent addition to Norman, as the franchise expands its fame for its signature burgers, such as the "Fatty." Customers enjoy a rock-and-roll aesthetic while they experiment with concoctions like peanut butter sweet potato fries and Alaskan fish burgers. Older patrons will remember the restaurant as a Coach's, but the corner of Main Street and Front Avenue (James Garner Avenue as of 2006) had as its most famous restaurant the unmatchable Denco's Café.

Denco's was the classic greasy spoon diner. From 1946 to 1981, people looking to fill their bellies without emptying their pockets came to sit at the counter or the tables, often pocked with old food. If patrons needed to go to

The site of Denco's and many other establishments in Norman.

the bathroom, they had to exit out a back door and go around the alley to another building that hosted the restroom plumbing.

Most of Denco's memories were made late at night, as it was one of the few places to stay open so late. When Norman's blue laws brought the bars to a close in the wee hours of the morning, Denco's was the place to be. Students were particular fans of the restaurant, which seemed to let them do anything they wished. Ketchup and salad dressing fights were known to erupt, and customers made a game of flinging pats of butter to see if they would stick to the ceiling. When the café closed in 1981, some of the pats were still clinging up there.

In the farewell article commemorating the passing of the diner, *Oklahoman* contributor Kevin Donovan wrote:

> *There are really two Normans. One of them is dominated by the University of Oklahoma satyrs and sorority girls, jocks and intellectuals. The other Norman is the "Run of '89" community, the natives whose families have lived in and around Cleveland County since the land was opened to the white man in the last century. Denco's was one place the two Normans seemed to meet each night.*

The meals of choice for the guests (in varying degrees of sobriety) were the Denco Darlin' and the Two Lookin' at You. The Denco Darlin' was a special chili served on top of elbow macaroni noodles, topped with Wisconsin cheese and an egg. The rest of the menu was straightforward counter café–style foods, but the most famous was the enchiladas, ordered as a pair with "dual enchies" or, for really hungry guests, "trip enchies." The Two Lookin' at You were enchiladas that had sunny-side-up fried eggs on top of them. Both were served on metal steak plates, most often seen today in Mexican restaurants with fajitas sizzling on top.

Opinions on the quality of the food varied. The trick to eating a Two Lookin' at You was to take a knife and fork and prop up the metal plate at an angle so the grease would pour out of the enchiladas. Some were disgusted by the thought of so much grease, while others said that it was part of the Denco's experience. Rumors circled that the cook put in extra Crisco just to make sure there was grease to pour off. More rumors had it that leftover chili was scraped back into the pot, where it would simmer with the rest for twelve hours.

Normanites absolutely loved the charm of the restaurant. In his history for the fraternity annual, Beta Theta Pi Jerry Kelley (class of '74) wrote, "No

Friday evening would be complete without a ride on the Denco train…Each is ready to drink in the Denco experience…Three Denco Darlin's, with Two Lookin' at You, together with a round of chips and green goddess dressing are quickly consumed."

Customers and proprietors alike enjoyed a laidback, adventure-filled lifestyle that attracted college students and Normanites ready for a cheap, easy meal. Denco's cook, Earl Bridgeford, described his chili as free from "onion, beans or tomatoes." Outside of that, the recipe was off-the-cuff. "We, Benny Flowers and I, just made it up." Customers were welcome to add anything they liked to their orders; most popular was to add a fried egg on top for an extra twenty cents. Show-offs might add two or even three eggs. Once the competition got started, the record for additional fried eggs weighed in at just shy of three dozen.

Older patrons would recall the site hadn't always served as a simple diner. Over the course of its more-than-a-century-long lifespan, the building had served as a bunkhouse for soldiers stationed to aid the territorial governor, a feed store and more. According to town legend, during the days of the navy base, the upstairs of the building hosted a brothel. After the war, as the Denco bus lines served Norman, Bennie and Eva Flowers turned it into a lunch counter and depot for the buses. The Denco buses stopped running in Norman in 1958, but Denco's Café kept on dishing up the Darlin's.

Denco's Café came to an end after thirty-five years, when the building was bought up by Charlie Newton and other businessmen who planned an $800,000 renovation to turn the restaurant into a swanky nightspot, including a rooftop garden and connecting the bathrooms to the main building. As Denco's closed up, old patrons began to become very nostalgic. There had been no previous announcement about the closing, and Newton was suddenly overwhelmed with cash offers for menus, plates and other memorabilia. The demand was finally settled at an auction, which partially funded the renovations. One enterprising former customer wasn't willing to wait for the auction and cut a section from the café's awning with Denco's scrawled out on it. Newton hired night watchmen to ensure no more pieces of history went missing.

The remodeling did not go as planned. Today, the building stands without its dreamed-of glass elevator and staircase out of *Gone with the Wind*. Some say that the renovations were scaled back due to costs, while others said that there was at least one ghostly patron that didn't want to see the building so changed.

The story of its ghost is perhaps best known to out-of-town guests who come after hearing legends from university alumni. Stories about the ghost

ALTHOUGH DENCO'S HAS CLOSED, nostalgia for tastier times continued on. In 1987, the Junior League of Norman put out a community fundraising cookbook known as the *Sooner Sampler*. To this day, the Junior League keeps Norman traditions alive through its hometown recipes in the newer *Simply Good Taste* book. The original '87 cookbook included a recipe for Darlin's that solidified the eyeballed measurements and cut out the MSG.

DENCO'S DARLIN

20 pounds chili meat
2¾ ounces paprika
2¼ ounces cumin
4 ounces chili powder
1 tablespoon garlic
1½ tablespoons cayenne pepper
1 cup salt
2½ tablespoons coarse black pepper
8 ounces jalapeno, ground
5½ ounces flour
5½ ounces salad oil
15 pounds elbow macaroni
12½ pounds cheddar cheese
100 eggs, fried

In a large pot, cover meat with water. Cook until meat completely breaks apart. Add paprika, cumin, chili powder, garlic, cayenne pepper, salt, black pepper and jalapeno and simmer for 30 minutes. Add roux mixture: 5½ ounces flour and 5½ ounces salad oil. Mix well. Cook macaroni until al dente.

For each serving, cover a hot platter with macaroni, ladle on enough chili to completely cover. Sprinkle 2 ounces of cheddar cheese on top and cook in convection oven for 6–8 minutes. Add fried eggs to taste. Serves 100.

The stairs to the second-floor office.

are as varied as the history of the building itself. Some long ago said that the ghost appears on the first floor as a vaguely human apparition, sitting in booths or at the counter. Others whispered that it was more menacing, overturning drinks and even flinging food across the room.

Staff working at S&B say that the ghost is generally limited to the stairs that go from the kitchen to the upstairs office. Plenty of people have been there late, wrapping utensils or closing, and have heard the clear sound of footsteps walking up and down the stairs. Sometimes, the steps begin at the top and traipse downward. Curious employees pause from their work and see who might have been sneaking around, but the kitchen stands empty of any living soul.

Other times, the steps begin on the first floor and walk up, dully thudding out one step at a time. Again, people rush to go see who is creeping around at night in the restaurant, and again no one is there to be seen. Some claim to have watched the stairs as the sounds creak one step at a time up the empty staircase. No one claims to have gone after them or tried to stop the invisible walker.

The identity of the ghost is often speculated about. People consider all points in the building's history, naming one employee or another who might still be skulking around the old store or stockade. More scandalous thinkers like to say the ghost comes from the days of the brothel, either as a client returning from the grave for a visit or a working girl who might have met a grisly end.

The most welcomed story for the ghost is as a customer at Denco's, still wanting a helping of a Darlin' and walking back and forth in search of a meal to die for.

BUMPS

S&J Marketplace

Antique shops universally offer a feeling of wonder and chilling awe. They are filled with items of another era, the personal possessions of people long gone. We are reminded of our own mortality when we venture into them, and more reflective patrons might wonder which of their valued objects will someday rest in shops for our children and grandchildren to see and grow nostalgic over.

Not all antique shops are scary, of course. Most, like the S&J Marketplace on Gray Street, have a charming air about them. Lovers of the old-fashioned come, like kids in candy shops, into rooms filled with the wonders of yesteryear. As they search through the rooms, they see books and toys from their childhoods. Collectors find memorabilia of cherished artists, musicians, actors and political icons or perhaps that final piece of china from their grandma's

Norman's old city offices.

wedding pattern. Others of us are bargain-hunters, seeking out furniture or kitchen tools that still carry great worth, though they have outlived their previous positions in homes, whether stately or humble.

S&J is known for its wide variety. Everything from old records and their players to framed works of art in every genre to dolls, dinnerware and furniture fill its rooms. Patrons flip through books, from decades-old first editions to recent bestsellers with dog-eared pages, ready for a new reader, each having its own musty scent of yellowing paper and sweet, faded ink. The air is cool and crisp, like a museum of our own lives.

A sense of claustrophobia may come over some patrons as they explore the many nooks of the market. Long hallways connect small rooms, many of which connect to one another to create a labyrinth. Compounding the feeling, the array of antiques covers the walls and shelves, often even the tabletops in the middle of the rooms. The building is surprisingly deep, stretching on and on with treasures.

In addition to its antiques and collectibles, S&J has another feature from the days when the building served as the city offices for Norman. In the 1960s, the offices moved to the new civic complex farther west on Gray Street, and the space transitioned into a small retail center. The confusing layout of S&J becomes clear when one realizes these small rooms were the offices for city workers in many departments. Some connected to others out of necessity, while others operated along the extended, narrow hallways.

Most impressive of all is the surviving office technology. Lights are operated from hidden switches for each room and sometimes rooms beyond. The utility closet still holds hundreds of telephone wires once used to connect the

Banks of phone lines still rest in the building.

many phones lines necessary to keep the city in working order. Each wire represents the ability of a citizen to call in, even if he or she had to be placed on hold. The switches direct the electrical currents onto new lines, filtering them through the whole building. The wire bank is an engineering feat and a testament to civil service.

Some patrons believe that there are former city employees still at work, even though the building has been converted and their bodies have long since passed to the grave.

Folks working at the S&J Marketplace, as well as their customers, have long heard bumps in the shop. The sounds typically come from the back of the shop, but sometimes they happen in the occupied room. People hear the noise of something falling or being shifted and look up to see no one at all.

Parapsychologists routinely link the presence of ghostly activity to places that were filled with emotional strain or significance. With the pressures of civic duty, it is no wonder that a spirit, so used to returning to work day after day, would be disturbed from eternal rest and come in to the office. As their incorporeal bodies stride around what were once desks and cabinets of papers, they bump into objects that, in their minds, should not be there.

Other patrons wonder if it isn't the building that has attracted strange activity but something in it. Just as certain sites might bring back those who were attached to it in life, so objects can become magnets for those who have passed. A doll cherished in life will still be cherished in the afterlife, and sometimes, even death cannot stop its owner from coming back to it.

Just like haunted houses, haunted objects have become so fascinating to popular culture that television programs and museums have been created to show them. Most of the items in museums are locked behind glass, not only to maintain them, but also to keep guests away, under the notion that the spirits may leave the object to follow them home. Some of the most famous are dolls, such as Annabelle (who came to the attention of demonologists Ed and Lorraine Warren after tormenting girls to the point where they felt like prisoners in their own apartment) and Robert of Key West, Florida (who supposedly attacked a woman with a knife and now curses those who take photographs of him without asking permission). Other objects include mirrors, paintings and chairs that give strange sensations to all those around them.

Not all haunted objects are necessarily negative. A man once told me of his father's cigarette lighter, a prized possession with the Harley Davidson logo on it. After his passing, a family squabble about his possessions ended with a brother taking the lighter, even though it was clear the father wanted the man to have it. Despite replacing the flint and the fluid, the brother could not get the lighter to light. He finally ended up giving it to the man, who, on the first flick, brought up a foot-high burst of flame. The lighter was a great help for starting fires or lighting fuses for the Fourth of July, but it would refuse to give even a spark whenever he tried to light a cigarette.

Antiques hold secrets of the lives of owners past.

Again, he replaced the flint and the fluid, but it would simply not light. Any other time, it worked perfectly, so he decided that it was his father, who had died of lung cancer, telling him to quit. So, he did. He still carries the lighter with him today.

Whether it is something that has brought in an unseen force or the building itself, something supernatural seems to wander through the marketplace. Unseen hands sometimes overturn objects, but mostly it seems to be the bumping sound. It is softer than an intentional knock, just the familiar sound of something hitting a piece of table, a wall or a bookcase. There are no signs of pests that could be responsible for such clear sounds. Even more, the sounds are too big to be a simple mouse scratching.

In addition to the bumps, staff working at the S&J Marketplace note a strange feeling that comes over them from time to time. Even though they know the shop is empty and the camera monitors show no one around, they get the sensation of not being alone. It gets bad enough that they cannot help but walk back through the store from the front desk asking, "Is anyone there?" No one has answered back yet.

"It's just something you get used to," they say.

PEEPHOLES

Old Post Office

Basements have always been strange, foreboding places. Perhaps it is a sense of claustrophobia, cut off from the life-giving warmth of the sun and the free-flowing sky. Perhaps it is the difference in air, which rests still, wet and heavy beneath the ground. Or perhaps it is because of the similarity with being in a tomb—the dampness and cold of the earth.

The basement of the Elaine Fulton Hale Professional Development Center for Norman Public Schools was once believed to be haunted, though the spirits are said to now have quieted down. As people drive down Gray Street and pass the domineering building with its stone gargoyles, it is easy to believe such a place has secrets. Rumors circulate about more than just ghosts; hidden catwalks lead to peepholes throughout the building.

The building began its life as the first post office in Norman. Norman received mail through the railroad long before the national postal service ever came to the town. After the run, letters and packages were simply

Norman's original post office.

dropped off at the rail depot; customers could pick up the mail themselves or send couriers for it. A large cardboard box was set in the middle of the waiting room floor at the station for Normanites to come rummage through to find envelopes marked for them. This postal situation lasted over a month until D.W. Marquart was appointed postmaster. His daughters did most of the work, sorting the mail that arrived four times daily.

Over the next four decades, the post office of Norman would be found in various rented spaces around downtown. The position of postmaster was a political plaything. Every time the White House changed political parties, the postmastership changed hands as well. Finally, in 1930, the Republican administration of Herbert Hoover determined that Norman needed a formal facility for its mail. After all, the city population had already surpassed 9,600 that same year. A firm from Dallas won a $68,000 contract, and much of the work was doled out to local contractors, boosting the local economy during the somber days of the Great Depression.

What came out of the construction was one of Norman's most beautiful buildings. Designed in the Art Deco architectural style prominent in the 1930s, the building stands with geometric solidity that lends itself to the post office's grave impression. Gargoyles and carved symbols keep watch

A walled catwalk stands hidden in the ceiling.

over green marble columns guarding the main entrance. Gold-colored brick stands warm in the southern sun alongside enormous windows that flood the interior with natural light.

Inside, the post office boasts carved wooden trim. Many of the original wooden windows still stand between the long, narrow entry room, where customers picked up and dropped off mail, and the sorting floor, where postal employees managed it. The sorting floor is an enormous room, once lined with tables, where each letter was checked and deposited by hand. High ceilings are interrupted, through the middle, with what looks like a needlessly large air duct—a clumsy disguise for the secret catwalk.

Wooden stairs lead up to the small second floor, where the postmaster had his office and bathrooms, with swooping brass and porcelain from the Jazz Age. A door no different from that of the broom closet leads out of the well-lit landing and into a dark hallway that runs the length of the building. High above the sorting floor, this is where the postmaster and his managers crept to spy on their employees.

About every four feet along the long hallway, two sets of peepholes look down on the sorting floor. Long slits were shaped into the cast iron and fitted with glass covers, frosted with age. Without letting their employees know, managers could walk up and down the catwalk and peek through the glass to check their progress. For a better look, and even to overhear them, they could quietly raise up the covers.

To go even further in their snooping, about every six feet in the floor, peepholes have been drilled into the concrete. The long slits allow spies to look from side to side along the length of the building. Managers must have realized that someone could be up to something (or, perhaps worse,

Slit-like peepholes allowed managers to watch employees.

not busy) unseen beneath their feet. With the peepholes, a pedantic watchman could get down onto his hands and knees and take a long look into the blind spot below.

When Norman began its explosive growth after the completion of Interstate 35, the post office was one of many civil institutions that needed more space and was soon moved to the city office complex, farther west on Gray Street. The building was turned over to the Norman Public Schools, who turned it into a place to teach its teachers. Elaine Fulton Hale served as director of the Professional Development Center for twenty-seven years, after working in elementary education at Adams Elementary School. Before her tenure, she described a time when teachers were largely left with what they had learned in their own classrooms and getting their degrees. "The ongoing training for professional development was considered a one-day event in the summer, when an outside consultant was selected to give a presentation to educators," but that proved not to be good enough. Hale wanted to create a new "focus on student learning" in staff development. Today, the sorting floor is now broken up into cubical offices and small, open classrooms with computer classes, testing and classroom materials for the improvement of education in Norman.

Between its days as the post office and its new life as the Norman Public Schools Professional Development Center, the building stood in a period of mismatched uses. Its basement was used for storage and became filled with old Christmas decorations, music recordings on eight-track tapes and boxes of papers from a dozen different locations. The changing room for less fortunate students who tried on donated clothes still stands. Amid all of the boxes, something else was said to have come into the basement.

The basement is separate from the rest of the building, with its utilities between the stairs that lead up to the main rooms. Huge industrial boilers growl loud enough to deafen. Sump pumps wait for their pipes that lead down to the old foundation to give the signal before joining in with their own howls. Most staff members avoid the noise and go around the building to the side entrance, which was once used for local deliveries. Labyrinthine offices twist between the ground-level entrance and the boilers, each room once dedicated to a different manager or to sorting incoming mail into bags for postmen to deliver. Some rooms connect to two or three others for no visible reason; others lead into hallways with dead-ends.

Among these rooms, older staff said they had heard the sounds of shuffling feet, despite knowing they were the only ones in the basement at the time. Adults who came to the building as children remember knowing in their hearts that something dark prowled through those rooms. It was as if someone else was there, standing in a corner, watching, waiting.

Other sounds of footsteps and general thumps were heard in the catwalk above and on the stairs. Staff there rarely paid them any mind, thinking that it is an older building with plenty of sounds to make as it settles. In the basement, however, there was a definite feeling of not being alone. Few liked to go down there, even by themselves. When they had to, the air was unnaturally cold, and hairs stood up incessantly on the backs of their necks. There was always the sensation of being watched or of someone just around the corner. Over the years, as new renovations have been finished and staff worked to clean out all of the old storage, the odd feelings and stories of something in the basement have begun to fade.

Some like to speculate that the post office's ghost was an old manager, still at work keeping an eye on the business of the building. Now that much of the storage has been cleaned out, he does not lurk as he used to. Staff joke that it is good incentive to keep the place orderly and efficient, since they never know who might be watching.

II

HAUNTED HOUSES

As ghosts are usually believed to be spirits returning to sites that once held great significance for them, it is not unreasonable that they most often come home. Of course, these homes usually have new, living occupants, who may or may not be happy to have them. Just like the living, spirits seem to have a wide spectrum of behavior, from beneficial to harmful.

Every so often, after a ghost tour, a few guests stop me with stories of their own. One couple related to me a story about a house that seemed to have a female ghost that was very particular about guests. When certain friends came by, things would spontaneously fall off the walls and off shelves. Other times, faucets turned themselves on and drains pulled themselves tight, flooding the upstairs bathroom and creating a waterfall down the stairs. Most memorable of all was the time the man came home to find all of his living room furniture pushed up against the back door, as if to say it didn't belong in the house.

Another story was told about a special education teacher who experienced strange activity after one of her young students tragically passed away. For weeks, things started becoming more and more unexplainable. First, it was a strange feeling that ended with the woman's hair being pulled by thin air. The experience was so terrifying that she had to walk out of the house and wait in the yard until her husband came home. Curtains began to pull themselves back from the windows, not just fluttering under the air conditioning but actually moving up the rod. Later, the washing machine, an older model with dials above its basin, turned itself on. She and a friend watched while

Falls Cemetery, northeast of Norman.

an invisible force turned the dials and the machine started filling with water. Things came to a head when a stapler floated in midair, and she decided to have the house blessed. Sometimes things still move across tabletops, pushing themselves into piles, but the ghost is more manageable. In her best teacher's voice, the woman calls out, "All right, enough. Now stop that!" and, for a time, things go back to normal.

While some ghosts seem malevolent or playful, some are surprisingly helpful. A man was watching a football game when his dogs were at the back door wanting to go out. He was torn between his duties as a pet owner and as a fan, but he finally decided to let them out as soon as the commercials came on. Before he had a chance, the door opened wide, and the dogs dashed out barking. It then closed itself. When the dogs were done outside, the door once again opened up to let them through and then closed again.

A young man had a story of his own about getting a cup of ice water and then lying down for a nap. When he woke up, he discovered a ghost had stolen all his ice; only water was left in the cup. We both kept straight faces for nearly two seconds before cracking up with laughter.

Even though there are jokers out there, a surprising number of people have genuinely strange experiences that seem unexplainable by any other cause. People rarely volunteer their stories out of the blue, but once the topic has been raised, we share stories of visitors both seen and unseen.

LAST STOP

Main Street

"My grandfather's house has always had a creepy feeling," Lara Kelly says. "Creepy but welcoming. Even when it's strange, it feels safe."

The old house on Main Street stands just a few blocks east of downtown. It dates back to just after the Land Run, its architecture still showing the low-slung style of the turn of the century. White-painted, square, brick columns match the wooden siding while supporting a deep, shadowy porch. The roof quickly runs upward from there with two windows peeking out from a later addition. It is one of many homes like it on the block, but few others have as many tales of paranormal activity.

The family moved into the home in 1950. Just like any old house, it came with its own stories. Legends, whispered by the children, said there was a little boy who had died there some years before. Sally Austin, Lara's mother, moved into his old room. His spirit, at least, was still there.

Sally recalls a number of occasions waking up and seeing him standing in her room, watching her sleep. He never seemed to move much, just stood there and watched her sleep. She would hide under the covers, less afraid of him, more just wanting him out of her room.

Even during waking hours, Sally saw him in her closet. She sat in her room from time to time, reading or playing, and then sounds would start to ring out from inside. The room turned cold. Goosebumps settled over her arms. Sally listened for a while, hearing a ball bounce and the clothes shuffle on their hangers. Sometimes she went to investigate, and she would find the dark-haired little boy in the closet before he vanished.

The boy played outside of the closet, too. Sally worked diligently to keep her room clean, as per her parents' wishes. She piled toys in boxes in the closet every time she cleaned, and they would find their way back onto her floor without anyone else coming into the room. As frustrating as the toys were, it was nothing compared to the cabinet doors that opened and closed themselves. With no one in the kitchen, the sound of a cabinet opening up rang through the house. A few moments later, after about the time it would take to search through the house, the door shut itself again. If someone were in the kitchen, the doors opened and closed while they watched.

It wasn't just her room. Other members of the household heard strange noises from the basement. It was a large basement with several rooms inside, built in an older style with space for indoor laundry. Clotheslines stretched overhead from wall to wall, allowing the family to hang up their clothes to dry rather than having to take them outside, where Oklahoma winds might leave them with more dirt than when they started.

The clotheslines would rattle one at a time: ting-ting-ting. It was the same sound as a young hand running underneath them, playing them like a loose-stringed guitar. The children and even the mother would say, "Oh, it's the ghost!" Even their dog, Pug, whose tail had been clipped down by the father to keep him out of trouble, knew something was down there.

Sally's father, however, didn't believe in such things. He would dismiss the noise and say, "Oh, there's a cat down there."

No one ever saw a cat in the basement. The younger kids wondered how a cat got up six feet into the air along a bare wall to get to the clotheslines. Older kids knew it was best not to argue.

The little boy wasn't alone, either. Sally recalls time and again walking into her room to see a portly African American woman standing next to her bed. She blinked, and the woman was gone. Over and over, the woman appeared and disappeared without reason.

Another apparition was a teenage boy who seemed to walk up and down the stairs to the second floor, which had been a later addition to the house, built by Sally's father. The boy first appeared as legs and bare feet, walking eerily up and down without a body. Gradually his form appeared, and the children nicknamed him "Gilligan" because he wore a sailor's suit.

Lara's sister, who refused to go in the basement, refused to go upstairs as well. The parents tried to keep a sense of sanity to the family, especially her grandfather, who didn't believe in ghosts. One time when the family was gathered in the living room, he announced clearly, "There's no such thing as ghosts." Immediately in the next room, the light switch turned on. Everyone looked around, taking a headcount and finding everyone still there. No one else should have been in the house, yet someone was trying to confirm that a ghost was indeed there.

It wasn't an isolated incident. Another time, the mother was trying to console her unnerved children. "Oh, I don't believe in ghosts."

Behind her, a windmill music box started up playing its slow tune. It was the kind powered by a spring, wound up by hand and then playing until its spring runs out. The slow ditty played on, and the family decided not believing wasn't much of an option.

With all of the activity, it sometimes strained the family. One morning, the mother heard footsteps ringing on the stairs. They began at the top and stumped down, one step after the other: bang, bang, bang. The heavy footfalls made her think it was one of the older boys and called out, "What do you want for breakfast?"

No one replied.

She was perturbed, feeling ignored when she was trying to provide. Minutes passed. Eventually, the footsteps sounded again, and the son appeared in the kitchen.

"Well?" she demanded in anger.

The son was shocked. He said he had been asleep until just then.

Although the strange activity might cause confusion from time to time, it seemed to be harmless. In fact, it even had its benefits. Late one night, one of the older boys sneaked back into the house after a night partying with his friends. He had a little to drink, but he felt sure he could get away with it by sobering up before anyone else awoke. He slipped into bed and relaxed with his cleverness.

Suddenly, his bed shook. Something came out of the darkness and grabbed the footboard, shaking it as if to say, "This is not OK." The brother stumbled out of bed and fled downstairs to sleep on the couch. The next morning, he had to explain what he was doing out of his room. He didn't go out drinking again.

Other times, the ghostly commotion was consoling. After the family's Uncle Horace passed away, a new event began: the back door opened and closed itself, even on windless days. Locks undid themselves, the knob turned and the door opened. A moment later, just as long as it would take a person to walk through, it shut itself again. Everyone said it was Uncle Horace coming over for a visit, and the explanation felt right.

The activity continued when the next generation came along. Lara Kelly's clearest memory of her childhood in the house was on a day she spent with her mother, keeping her cousin Chad, who was sick in bed, company. She decided to get a snack and asked if Chad would like any bread and butter. He said no.

Lara went along to the kitchen alone and began slicing a loaf of homemade bread. Next to her, she saw a blond boy walk up. Chad was blond so she assumed it was him, and she teased, "Come to get some bread after all?"

The boy didn't answer. When she turned around to ask him again in case he didn't hear, the boy was gone.

Lara was shocked by her cousin's rudeness. When she went back to the bedroom, she demanded, "Why didn't you answer me?"

"Answer what?" Chad asked.

"In the kitchen," she said. She told him and her mother all about Chad walking up and then going off without giving her any notice.

Chad's face was blank. "That wasn't me. I was here the whole time."

Lara was again shocked. Yet her mother confirmed his story. "I was here the whole time, too."

As unnerving as the disappearing boy was, nothing scared Lara like the upstairs. At the landing on the stairs, there was a door that helped keep down noise and prevented hot air from pooling in the second-floor bedrooms. She was playing with her cousins, sneaking off from one another in an informal game of hide-and-seek. For fun, she knocked on the door as if she was asking to come in.

Someone knocked from the other side.

Lara grinned. She knocked again, this time in two beats.

Someone knocked back with the same two beats.

She knocked twice again, and as soon as the person on the other side gave one knock, she threw open the door. No one was there.

Lara ran down the stairs. It was a long time before anyone could convince her to go upstairs again.

Other family members witnessed odd happenings, too. Lara came over one day to spend some time with her grandmother. They were home alone, sitting in the front living room and talking when suddenly the old Victrola stereo in the back parlor began to play.

"Go see who that is," Granny told her.

Lara shook her head. "No way!"

Finally, the two decided to investigate together. They crept into the parlor and found the stereo's lid up and a record playing. No one living was there. While they watched, the lid slammed itself shut and the music stopped.

Lara and her grandmother ran back into the living room, as quickly as her grandmother's eighty-nine-year-old legs could carry her. Lara described the encounter in the parlor as disconcerting but not terrifying. They fled out of embarrassment as much as out of fear. Whoever started the music seemed just as surprised and embarrassed.

Over the course of the strange years, family members tried to determine why their house seemed to be so haunted. Sally Austin recalled, "I don't remember seeing anything until the upstairs was built." She wondered if something might have been stirred up by the construction.

Others noted that the house was near a cemetery and thought of it as a last stop before spirits went on. The story of Uncle Horace and later commotions were references to other family members who had recently passed.

After Lara's grandmother passed away, the activity seemed to quiet down. Her grandfather still lives in the house and denies that it is haunted. Even announcing he doesn't believe in ghosts doesn't seem to stir up any response.

Reflecting on the quiet rather than the noises, the family wonders if it wasn't the mother and her daughters attracting the spirits. The women in their family, going back for generations, seemed to have a special connection with the paranormal. Often it was seen as a blessing, an assurance of the afterlife, but the gift also made any dark presence much darker.

BAD HOUSE

Branchwood Drive

Sally Austin and Lara Kelly's maternal ancestors have a long history of having a special closeness with the spiritual. Their family came to Oklahoma out of Arkansas, where they had lived since the early 1800s. Austin recalls an aunt who, as a young girl in Arkansas, sometimes saw a dog with a man's head walk through the dogtrot in the middle of the family cabin. Soon after, someone near them would die. It happened on at least three horrifying occasions.

Lara's great-great-great-grandmother had the mystical ability of healing through her faith. She underlined several passages in the family Bible that she read over the injured to stop their bleeding. People from all over were brought to her, or she was called to them.

When Sally's mother was on her deathbed in the hospital, she twiddled the sheets in her hand, as if she were waiting. Suddenly, she looked up happily and announced, "There they are!"

Everyone looked around. No one new had come into the room. "Who are, Mom?"

"The family," she said. "They finally found Horace. And there's a little boy I don't know." The family was surprised by the boy but later recalled her brother Pete, who had died of a childhood illness before she was born.

The tradition continues. Both Sally and Lara laugh when they tell the story of the birth of Lara's daughter Lilly. When Lara was pregnant, the phone rang one morning, earlier than Lara would have liked.

It was Sally. "I had a dream. Granny says Lilly's birthday is October 1."

Lara, already cranky, wasn't amused.

When October 1 rolled around, the family was over visiting Lara's grandfather. They were gathered in the living room of the house that had been the setting for so many ghost stories. The activity had calmed down after her grandmother's death. The only strange happening Lara remembered was seeing a gray-haired woman walk from the living room into her grandmother's bedroom. She thought it was her mother until Sally came out of the kitchen from the opposite direction.

On October 1, the strangeness was back. As the family chatted, the front door suddenly flew open. Just as suddenly, it slammed shut again. No wind gusted.

"Well, somebody's come to visit!" Lara's grandfather joked.

Before anyone could reply, Lara's water broke. Two and a half hours later, Lilly was born.

Outside of the old family house, Sally and Lara have a number of strange stories stemming from times they have visited cemeteries on Memorial Day through the years. On one occasion, Lara recalls seeing an older man standing over a grave, pacing and looking tortured. He wore a London Fog coat and a hat her grandfather might have worn.

"I can't believe I let this happen," he was muttering to himself. "I can't play ball with Tommy now. Oh, Tommy, Tommy…"

Lara was devastated, feeling on the verge of hysteria. She whispered to her mother, "Do you see him?"

"No," her mother said, her breath short, "but I feel something."

It gave Lara the sad sense of a grandfather departed too soon.

While the spirits that affect the family often seem to be humans who have passed on, sometimes something darker attaches to them. Driving past a cemetery on Highway 9 one afternoon, Lara had a sudden feeling of illness. At the same time, her car seat pressed at her back, as if someone were kicking it from the backseat.

The feeling continued even after she arrived home. Something felt wrong about the house. Lara's husband, who often shrugs off her encounters with the paranormal, felt something was wrong and asked her pointblank, "What is that?"

Lara didn't know exactly, but she said she'd deal with it in the morning. It had been a rough day, and it was a rough night. Lilly didn't want to sleep in her bed. "There's something evil in my room."

The next day, they cleansed the house with prayer, cedar, sage and scented oil. Things went back to normal in the usually cheerful home.

As awful as the thing that followed her home was, the house Lara grew up in on Branchwood Drive was worse, and there was no simple cleansing to be rid of it.

The family moved into the house thinking it was a godsend. It was a charming brick house, and the price was surprisingly low, perfect for a a young widow and her two girls. They didn't think much of it being one of those houses that seem to always be on the market, despite there being nothing physically wrong with it.

There was something else wrong with the house. Just after they finished moving in, Sally came back from an errand to find the front window completely covered by a swarm of black flies. Their buzzing was deafening as they crawled over one another, seemingly eager to get through the glass. She dealt with the flies and didn't think too much of it, but that was only the beginning of the problems with the house.

Decorations and boxes that were stored in the attic constantly went missing. After diligent searches, they would find what they were looking for moved into other boxes or on the opposite side of the room. Sally asked the children if they had been up in the attic, but the kids replied that they never went up there, even if they wanted to. No one went into the attic, yet things kept moving.

The front bedroom was turned into a playroom for the children. Sally recalls on a number of occasions being called by her kids: "Would you come in here? He doesn't come out when you're here!"

"Who?"

The children didn't know how to describe him. He was just a mean presence that would watch them.

The haunting was worst at night. Scratching sounds came from the ceiling and walls, especially in the bedrooms. They weren't constant like the scratching of vermin, and exterminators found nothing. Lara remembers sleeping with the radio on to drown out the skrtch-skrtch-sktrch. Sometimes it got so loud she just had to leave and go sleep in another room. When she stayed, she often awoke to feel the covers being pulled off of her.

Both at night and during the day, the sound of voices yelling joined in. Lara recalls clearly hearing the yells, but they were never distinct enough to tell what the words were. Another voice, that of a young girl, did call out unmistakably, "Mom!"

The Austins didn't know much about the history of the house, but it seemed to carry the shades of an argument years before. They weren't the only ones to feel it, either. Sally bumped into the previous owner at the store later, and the woman was shocked. "You're still there?"

The family didn't stay in the house much longer. Even driving by it years later, they still shudder at the bad memories.

It Came Through the Window

Charles Burnell lived for a few years in a mobile home at the edge of a park in Noble. It was a sizeable trailer with a couple of extra bedrooms that he could rent out to roommates to supplement his income as a barista. He had lived there for quite some time with no problems, but then strange things began happening in December 2012.

It started when Charles was dog sitting for a friend over the holidays. When she dropped the dog off, they chatted and she turned on the TV to have something going in the background. They talked for a while before she had to leave, and then Charles said goodbye, turned off the TV and went back to his bedroom. Suddenly the dog began barking, yapping and crying so much it could barely catch its breath.

Charles came back in the room to see what was the matter. The TV was on again. The dog stood growling, staring at nothing. No one else was there.

He wondered whether his friend had come back. "Is anybody there? Are you playing a trick on me?"

No one replied.

Charles shrugged it off. He assumed the dog had gone nutty from seeing his owner leave and must have stepped on the remote control. Charles turned off the TV.

A cold sensation immediately came over him, like a winter wind passing right through him. It left him as quickly as it had come. He felt he wasn't alone.

The dog continued to stare just past Charles.

It was an odd event, but Charles said he didn't think too much of it. He said he believes in the supernatural, but he "isn't one to see ghosts." He knew people who claimed to see ghosts, but he never saw what they did, so he never worried much about it.

After the New Year, Charles had family come to stay—his cousin and her son, whom Charles considered a nephew. The eleven-year-old immediately described the ghost of an "old Indian granny" that lived in the house. Meanwhile, Charles's cousin's phone began suffering glitches. It deleted items, turned itself on and off and would ring with no one calling. Its battery was constantly dying. They blamed bad service in the area, but a few weeks later, when the cousin and her son moved into a house two doors down, the phone was fine.

Another guest soon arrived: Charles's goddaughter. Although she was not even old enough to drive, she seemed to have a gift for communicating with the supernatural, being "very in touch with spirits." It was as if they were attracted to her, seeking help with their problems in the afterlife.

Charles and his goddaughter sat on his bed playing cards one evening when something appeared in the window. Charles had noticed problems with his window in the weeks before. The blinds had broken in the middle as if someone had been pushing them apart with enough force to crease the plastic. Charles had thought someone was climbing through, but his desk sat right below it and nothing had been moved. Moreover, the window didn't open. It was a pane set into the wall.

That night, Charles and his goddaughter both noticed the thing shining in the dark. He described it as a little turquoise light, blindingly bright and growing as it came directly toward them. Charles thought it was a car with one headlight out, but its path was so straight that it came though the trees. Its shape became more distinct; it had a rich blue center and a white edge as it came to the window. When it passed through the glass and disappeared, Charles's phone beeped from where it was resting on the edge of the bed.

It was a new phone, one he had just gotten since his old one had suffered problems similar to his cousin's. When he picked it up, he saw that it had taken a picture. Without anyone to pick it up, the camera app had activated, snapped a shot and turned itself off. It was the first picture taken on the new phone, and it showed the corner of his room with the window. Coming through the glass, not merely on it—was a blue-white glare.

Later, Charles would try to go back and re-create the photo. At the same time of night with the same lights on, he tried angle after angle to find a similar reflection on the window. To make a glare like the one that night, though smaller and lighter, he had to stand on his bed and press the phone against the wall. Whatever it was in the picture, it wasn't natural light. He's kept the photo, though phones and computers it has been stored on have regularly given out.

The thing that had come into the room gave both Charles and his goddaughter a very nervous feeling. It was a climax to the strange sounds, electrical problems and unexplainable cold drafts that had been building up over the weeks. As he told his family and friends about the events, their growing interest only attracted more strange activity. Charles was done with it.

He stood and announced clearly, "You are not allowed to come into the house!"

The feeling was gone. As days passed, the strange noises stopped sounding through the house. The problems with the television and cellphones ceased. Whatever had been plaguing the house, it was over.

Since the odd winter months of 2012–13, Charles has reflected on what exactly the presence was that haunted his home. He passed around copies of the weird photo—the "very first picture taken on the phone, and I didn't take it"—to friends for their thoughts, but he stopped after phones and computers that had the image began wiping their own memories and corrupting their operating systems.

"It didn't like electronics," Charles notes. He is reminded of the thoughts of Nikola Tesla, who described "ghostly" activity as ambient electricity. With our modern sensitive electronics, "Something with electrical force passing through could make it glitch."

Even if it were just a natural electrical phenomenon, he does not feel that it was mindless. After all, it stopped when he asked.

CAR DOORS

132nd and Old Highway 9

Before the area east of Norman was Lake Thunderbird State Park, it was farmland—the best farmland in the county, according to Bob Oliphant, whose father bought a farm there in the late 1920s. With high prices (due to World War I) and bountiful crops, agriculture was a lucrative business to the recently settled region. Bob's grandfather had done well enough on his farm to help set up his son-in-law, George Smith, in a bank and buy a house in Noble for his children to live in during the school year rather than having them travel an hour over dirt roads each day.

The war ended, and demand for American crops collapsed as Europe rebuilt. The recession was made worse by a severe drought in the 1920s that would lead to the Dust Bowl. Many farmers gave up and either moved to town or migrated to greener pastures, famously to California as Okies. O.B. Oliphant and his brother Dee were determined to buy the land cheap and wait out the drought in the weather cycle. Farmers are a patient breed, and O.B.'s gamble paid off when demand again skyrocketed with World War II.

The land already had a colorful history. A man who had scouted out a prime section in the days before the run in 1889 staked it. When the noon cannon fired on April 22, he spurred his thoroughbred horse off the eastern line in Pottawatomie territory. He arrived at the claim he wanted, only to find a man already plowing with a team of horses that had been unhitched from his wagon. Not only had a wagon somehow outraced a single rider, but his team was also fresh enough to begin fieldwork. Despite the suspicious situation, all the man could do was head back to claim a section nearby that was bisected by the Little River.

As a youngster in the 1950s exploring around the farm, Bob stumbled upon a pile of old rusted pipes and tubs hidden in the blackjack oaks. He asked his father about it, and all O.B. would say was: "There was an old still up there." It dated back to the early days of Prohibition, one of many installations in the backwoods of Oklahoma sidestepping Washington's laws. The firebox had a forced draft system with a bellows that O.B. said could be heard for miles when it ran, but locals weren't terribly worried about federal investigations.

In 1942, with the war effort in full swing, O.B. bought an old church building as a new house for his family. It was a Holy Roller church, one of the many branches of Charismatics who settled near Seminole. Their communities suffered along with the rest, and ultimately this church broke up, enabling O.B. to buy and move the church. It arrived as a big open hall, and the family divided it into bedrooms and living space by putting up new inside walls. The partitions made a house two rooms wide and three deep, with a shed room at the back. It was a cleverly engineered building, like two shotgun houses added together.

The new house also came with something unusual: the unexplainable sound of car doors slamming. They began inexplicably in the 1950s as slams sounding exactly like someone shutting a car door. The banging seemed to happen most often during the summertime, ringing out over the chirping cicadas and hot Oklahoma wind. There was no precursor sound of an engine, nor were there signs of tire tracks afterward.

Time and again, family members would be in the house and hear the familiar sound of car doors banging shut. They would get up, open the front door and find the yard empty. The older kids ignored it. The younger kids were perplexed and wondered about haunted woods.

Even guests heard the slams. A friend of Bob's older brother was visiting when the doors sounded. He got up to go see who it was, and they said not to bother. "No one's there." The friend was perplexed. He didn't know whether to be more surprised by inexplicable car doors or by how accustomed the Oliphants had gotten to the phenomenon.

Even O.B., a pragmatist who had little time for the supernatural, noted the doors. He joked that it was indeed the sounds of the dead. "One of the Holy Rollers has passed away, and that's the hearse."

The explanation was a solid one. The farmhouse was isolated on a dead-end road. Others have suggested gunfire, but rural Oklahomans have hunted enough to know the difference between a shot and a car door.

Instead, the family holds to the explanation of Holy Rollers bidding a final farewell to a building that hosted so many of their services. If it were elder members of the former congregation passing away, it seems sensible that more of them would pass away in the summer, in a time before air conditioners became common.

When the land was purchased by the Bureau of Reclamation, for the construction of Lake Thunderbird, the house was auctioned off to a family who moved it to Cedar Lane. Years later, the new family living there swore it was haunted. They did not hear any car doors, but they did have a man in overalls who would appear in the corner of their eyes. As soon as they caught a glimpse, he was gone.

FIGURES IN THE NIGHT

In addition to the mysterious slamming car doors, the church house that became a farmhouse was the scene of what Bob Oliphant described as the scariest moment of his young life. He said it was "the first time I truly felt afraid."

At about eleven years old, he was awakened in his bed by the sound of footsteps walking in the kitchen. The back door did not open, nor were there any steps coming in; they simply began with a step in the middle of the kitchen, "as if someone had just turned on a radio." He lay in bed and listened as the footsteps moved.

The footsteps plodded one after the other, growing louder and louder as they came through the living room and into his room. Then they stopped.

The moment seemed to last an eternity as whatever it was stood there. Bob was too afraid to look up, though he could feel a presence just behind him.

Finally, it began to walk again, and the floorboards creaked as it went on its way back into the kitchen. Then it stopped, turned around and walked back into Bob's room. Again he refused to look, fearing he might not see anything at all. He didn't want to acknowledge it, feeling it was something fragile that would disappear if he surprised it. The footsteps walked out of his room again, back to the kitchen and ceased.

The Black Figure has appeared in stories related to me from a number of sources that have no way of knowing one another. It is always described in the same way. The storyteller is absolutely certain it was a tall man, but he or she is unable to give distinctive details, except for the eyes, which are sometimes red and sometimes white. In the majority of the stories, the Black Figure is simply passing through, walking inexplicably from one place to the next and pausing only momentarily to trade long looks.

In one story told to me by a waitress who said she often (and unfortunately) saw strange visions, the Black Figure was at rest. She awoke to find someone all in black hugging her boyfriend next to her, with its arms draped around his neck. In her sleep-addled mind, she thought it was her boyfriend's roommate pulling another silly stunt, so she moaned and said, "Sam, get off of John!"

The figure rose up. It wasn't Sam.

As in the other stories, the Black Figure was lanky and shadowy. It stood tall, leaning under the ceiling over the bed. It raised up its arms with a gesture she didn't understand, whether asking forgiveness or threatening her. Before she could say anything, it was gone.

Another specter that haunted the waitress was white and shorter, something of an opposite of the Black Figure. She heard noises in the kitchen and walked in to see who was cooking. An all-white figure with folds over its face, like it was wearing a hoodie, was busily going through the drawers. It pulled them open one after the other, rustling through the silverware and cooking utensils.

She hurried out of the kitchen to grab her boyfriend. "I saw someone in the kitchen!"

He didn't believe her, like the time she had seen ghostly children, a boy and an older sister, pulling clothes out of their dresser and giggling. This time she insisted that he get up and go with her.

When they came back into the kitchen, the white figure was still there going through the drawers. This time it seemed to notice them coming in, and it turned around as if startled. Its eyes glowed brighter and brighter under its folds, and then it, too, disappeared.

Not all of the stories have inexplicable creatures that are visible or heard; others seem simply *felt*. A man had inherited a house with some wooded land east of town, a place he had loved when he grew up and now used as a space to entertain. He hosted cookouts, parties and quiet affairs where old friends could sit around the campfire and tell stories into the night. On one of those nights, something evil arrived.

It was a summer in the mid-1970s, and friends were gathered in the living room trying to stay cool in an old house without air conditioning. Suddenly, an icy chill swept over the room. Rather than being comforted, everyone there felt a sense of horror. For a long time, no one spoke, and then they all asked simultaneously, "Did you feel that?"

Whatever it was gave a new vibe to the old place. It began to squelch good feelings, and arguments popped up from nowhere among old friends. The man decided he'd had enough and went about his own way to cleanse the malevolent spirit that had come to inhabit the place—stripping it to the rafters and redoing the whole house. Through the years, he has made a conscious effort to return the house to a place that would make his uncle proud. Whenever a negative feeling seemed to be trickling in, he redecorated and remodeled to keep it out.

The efforts seem to have paid off. Recently, the house served as a temporary home for tornado victims. They noted how it felt like a "place of healing." He aims to keep it that way.

III

MORE HALLOWED HALLS

The University of Oklahoma started alongside the rest of the territory, following the Land Run of 1889. The territorial legislature wanted to be culture to the wilderness of the prairie, and Norman was selected on the conditions it could raise $10,000 in cash to start the school and a $5,000 bond to ensure the sale of forty acres of land for a campus. Normanites came together enthusiastically to raise funds for the school, though there was a squabble about whether the campus should be on the east or west side of town. Using their contacts within the railroad, the west-side players, headed by Delbert L. Larsh, found out when the territorial selection committee was to arrive and met it at the station to take the committee members to their favored site, where the university stands today.

While there was money and an eager board of regents, it was no easy task to build up an institute of higher education from the prairie sod. The first hire was David Ross Boyd, the superintendent of schools in Arkansas City, Kansas. Under his tenure there, an impressive new building had been constructed with an equally impressive state-of-the-art heating system. In July 1892, Boyd was invited to speak to the regents about his heating system. After his presentation, he was blindsided by the invitation to become OU's first president and professor of mental and moral science. Boyd's first class of students would be arriving in two months, and he had no classroom building, no faculty other than himself and nowhere to house his students.

Boyd was up to the challenge. Earlier that year, the first university hall had begun construction, under Charlie Holcraft, who worked to finish the

Main Street during the cotton harvest. *Courtesy Cleveland County Historical Society.*

building even though the project had run out of money halfway through. In the meantime, Boyd found classroom space on the second floor of the Adkins-Welch Rock Building on West Main Street, rented at $20.00 per month. Meanwhile, Boyd grabbed up the first faculty to include chemist Edwin C. DeBarr; linguist William N. Rice; and professor of English, history and civics French Amos, who joked that he had been hired because his father was a regent's neighbor. They arrived two weeks before classes started. Boyd himself was living at the Agnes Hotel. From there, he sent out advertisements to the city asking for families to house and board students at $2.50 a week. Normanites gladly volunteered their homes. On September 15, 1892, classes at the University of Oklahoma began in downtown Norman, with fifty-seven students.

Since that time, the university has moved to its current location—once the cornfield of '89er Charles Gorton—and expanded rapidly. After a few false-starts, with devastating fires that destroyed OU's only buildings twice, the campus has filled up with buildings for science, law, engineering and the arts. Rapid expansion of the student body has brought an entire city's worth of dormitories and a sprawling student union with athletic facilities to match. With so many people having gone through the campus, it is no wonder a few of them come back to visit from beyond the grave.

In *Campus Ghosts of Norman, Oklahoma*, I collected all of the stories I had heard and researched for the ghost tour, which began with a single story about a roller-skating ghost boy. Since then, I have been surprised again and again by the number of ghost stories in the many buildings on and around the campus of the University of Oklahoma. Shadows roam bygone buildings, fraternities and former dormitories are bustling and a professor of art won't let a simple thing like death keep him from overseeing the growth of our culture.

THE THIRD FLOOR

Rhyne Hall

While no longer standing, Rhyne Hall was once a mysterious building that rested on the eastern edge of campus, past even the roars of the facilities management compound and the dutiful engineers in their shops. It was a large, yellow-brick building with a crimson tile roof that stood out among the parking lots. Its Spanish architecture—popular in the 1920s—with sections set at different depths, as if they had been added later, seemed out of place among the Cherokee Gothic of the campus. Students who ventured inside found it filled with spacious downstairs rooms and creaking wooden staircases that led up to cramped offices. Many students wouldn't dare set foot in the building because of the rumors that it was haunted.

The men of the Alpha Tau Omega fraternity were the first to inhabit the building. The organization started in September 1865, at the Virginia Military Institute. With the wounds of the Civil War struggling to heal, the founders sought a way for brotherly love to bring Americans back together in peace. In 1880, founder Otis Allan Glazebrook wrote a creed for his younger brothers, "to know no North, no South, no East, no West, but to know man as man." ATO colonized OU in 1921, as fraternities raced to expand over the nation's campuses. By 1928, they built the house that would serve as the fraternity's home for decades, until it moved to a larger house west of campus.

The university purchased the building and granted it to the School of Social Work, which up to that time had its offices in the basement of Adams

Rhyne Hall as it once stood.

Hall, the business building. In 1977, it was named in honor of Dr. Jennings J. Rhyne, who had joined the faculty fifty years before. He began as a professor of sociology, but within a year had become director of the Department of Social Service, which soon became the School of Social Work. While he stepped down as director in 1950, he continued on as professor until his retirement in 1967, after forty years of dedication. Through his time and afterward, the School of Social Work expanded rapidly to integrate graduate degrees and new relationships with community groups.

Even after his retirement, Rhyne continued to contribute to the school. He was a prolific writer, observing the trials of the day and offering understanding to best support the nation. In 1929, his *Social and Community Problems of Oklahoma*, described the impact of better roads and new technology to the young state. He predicted the end of small towns as farming communities: "Everywhere there is evidence of the lessening importance of the village trading center in the economic and social life of the farmer…[who] comes to see the advantage of transporting his goods to a larger trading center." Lifestyles, too, were changing: "It is no longer necessary for the farmer to go to a church to hear a sermon. He can sit comfortably in his home and hear over his radio a sermon of a noted divine in a distant city." While the world was becoming all the more interconnected, he feared the end of the tightly knit neighborhood and sought ways to restore what was quickly becoming lost.

Students rarely ventured upstairs in Rhyne Hall, where staff and faculty were known to have strange encounters. Custodian Sheryl Campbell feels sensitive to paranormal activity and always had a nervous feeling about the upstairs. One day while cleaning, she saw a shadowy figure appear in the hallway. It seemed impossibly dark, like a nebulous entity of evil. She hurried downstairs and refused to go up there again unless someone went with her.

Others had weirder, though less threatening, confrontations that seemed to center on the third-floor bathroom, which gave a notorious unsettled feeling. Dr. David Moxley had his office on the third floor across from "that despicable restroom." He had heard stories of graduate students seeing people wandering down the hallway and then disappearing, but he filed them alongside the same joking rumor that he had set up a colony of hobos in the basement by inviting some of the school's less fortunate partners to stay where it was warm and dry before they could get settled in a shelter.

Late one night, about 1:00 a.m., while grading papers and finishing up work, Dr. Moxley happened to look up to see a man float down the hallway. The vision was vivid: a man in his fifties, looking like a fellow who had lived a rough life, a heavy smoker and a heavy drinker. He was tall and lanky, malnourished like death itself. The man turned toward Dr. Moxley, making eye contact, and then eased into the bathroom, backing through the door.

What struck him as odd most of all, aside from it being one o'clock in the morning, was that the man didn't amble as he walked, moving his shoulders as people do when they put one foot in front of the other. He just moved in place.

After a few minutes of trying, Dr. Moxley couldn't shake the stranger from his mind. He got up and went into the bathroom to check on him.

The room was empty.

Dr. Moxley checked each of the stalls, looked back into the hallway to see if he had slipped out somehow and still found nothing. He stood confused for a moment and then decided to head home. It would be a long while before he worked late again.

In 2011, the School of Social Work was moved to Zarrow Hall, a brand-new building at 700 Elm Avenue that replaced the old Tri Delta sorority house. The creaky, aged Rhyne Hall was torn down and replaced with parking to serve the growing campus. Faculty, staff and students are much more comfortable with their new surroundings, free from hauntings, though it was, oddly enough, the site of an exorcism in 1973. Despite the stories of their old building and the history of 700 Elm, staff and faculty at Zarrow Hall report no strange activity other than the elevator sometimes starting itself up to go to different floors.

RESIDENTS

Robertson and Hester Halls

The University of Oklahoma began without dormitories, but it was soon clear that students needed more than boardinghouses and a few fraternities to call home. The most crucial group of students that the administration sought to serve was its young women. They had lived in boardinghouses and a few communal homes that had been set up by different denominations, such as the Catholic Newman Hall on Boyd Street, but they sought a new level: on-campus housing.

As a progressive institution on the frontier of America, the University of Oklahoma did not have dour administrators citing tradition as excuses not to admit women. Instead, President Boyd, eager to have all the willing minds he could find, actively sought out female students. Women, often surprised that they would be encouraged to higher education, flocked to the university. Fantene Samuels became the university's first female graduate in 1901. About that same time, Grace King, OU's first female faculty member and originator of the colors crimson and cream, became the first professor of music at sixteen years old. Over the next century, the impact of women continued to grow in every department. Today, graduating classes are beginning to boast more female students than male.

In 1925, the campus completed its first dormitories. Both were designated for young women, and both were named after historical figures in Oklahoma's past. One was name after Elizabeth Fulton Hester, who—after completing her degree and even serving as faculty at Southern Masonic Female Seminary in Covington, Georgia, by the age of seventeen—came to Indian Territory in the 1850s as a missionary to the Choctaw and Chickasaw. She served as a teacher to Indians, whites and African Americans and a clerk in her husband's dry goods store. She was also a nurse in the hospital that she turned the store into during the Civil War, hosting injured soldiers from the Battle of Middle Boggy Depot and even Quantrill's Raiders. The other dormitory was named after Ann Worcester Robertson, who came to the

Robertson Hall, on the west side of Elm Avenue.

territory as a missionary on the Trail of Tears. She worked in the Creek Nation, translating the whole of the New Testament and much of the Old, complicated linguistics work that earned her an honorary doctorate from Wooster College in 1892. Her daughter Alice Mary went on to serve as Oklahoma's first congresswoman, elected in 1921.

For the next four decades, hundreds of young women shared living space on the east side of Elm, just a little south of the infirmary, eventually called Ellison Hall, after the first dean of student health. OU's image archives contain numerous pictures of female students in lounges playing cards, holding club meetings and studying in the privacy of their own dormitories. The rooms were small but cozy, designed with the same classy brickwork in the Cherokee Gothic style that became famous on campus.

With the completion of Cross Center as new dormitories for co-eds in the 1960s, Robertson and Hester Halls were turned into offices for various departments throughout the university. Through the years, the drama school, religious studies, women's studies, the graduate school and parking services have all occupied the dorm. The university bookstore, now in the stadium complex, once occupied the whole first floor and spacious basement of Hester.

The new lives of the buildings have also come with shades of the past. The most famous activity is the footsteps in the halls. Many staff members have stayed late to finish up work and heard someone walking down the hall. In the quiet of the night, the footfalls are clear, one at a time, padding

The halls where student spirits are said to walk.

from one end to the other. Further, the motion sensor lights flick on, just as they would with anyone walking through. Curiosity drives late-night workers to get up and peek into the hall, but they always find it empty. Despite the sounds and the lights, no living soul is to be found.

Certain rooms in Robertson have unique paranormal activity. In the graduate student lounge, on the third floor, the bathroom is famous for turning its lights on and flushing its own toilet. Like many of the toilets on campus, theirs are automated by infrared sensors, while the lights have motion detectors that switch off when no one is around. Something, however, seems to prowl in the lounge, where the sensitive electronics are able to pick it up. At all hours of the night and day, too random to be a programmed error, something causes the lights to flash and shine. The toilet gives its roar, despite no one being in the room. Workers try to keep the door closed to avoid the noise and flashing distractions, but it seems to open all by itself.

On the second floor, the northernmost office is famous for being cold. Most people tease the woman working there for simply being "cold-blooded" and especially sensitive to the chilly vents. Others who have been in the office agree that it is unnaturally frigid. The general consensus around the floor is that the office must be the closest to the air conditioner, although there isn't an office especially warm at the opposing end, nor does it explain why the cold continues in the winter, despite the heater turning on. Parapsychologists often describe "cold spots" as places where ghosts absorb thermal energy from the mortal realm (adhering to the Law of Conservation) to make the sounds of footsteps or move enough to be sensed by electronic machines. The woman has never herself experienced any movement or sounds in the office, where she has spent countless hours bundled under a blanket with a space heater tucked under her desk.

The first floor has its own strange disturbances: voices. Every so often, a voice, described as female and distant, calls out among the offices of women's studies. Most of the time, the voices are dismissed as someone from outside or the remodeling in Hester Hall, but others are not so easily explained away. A student worker, serving as a secretary, heard someone call out her name, specifically asking for her. She came down the hall to the head secretary's office and the study lounge. No one had heard any call for her.

Opinions are split among the officemates in Robertson about whether the building is actually haunted or simply "old, with plenty of character." While creaking floors might emulate footsteps and a cold office could be ventilation issues, the constant activation of motion sensors makes people wonder if there aren't things unseen moving through the old dorm. Believers

A set of winding stairs used by college coeds for forty years.

say the ghosts are the girls of Robertson and Hester, back to visit a place they treasured in their lifetimes, now ended. Whatever the activity is, it certainly seems conscious as it calls out to the living.

LOST BROTHER

Phi Kappa Psi

Directly across Elm Avenue from Hester and Robertson Halls is the Phi Kappa Psi fraternity, which began at Jefferson College in Canonsburg, Pennsylvania, in 1852. Typhoid struck Jefferson in 1850, and many students fled. Classes were called off, and the school was threatened to be closed down, but a few students stayed on to keep it open. William Letterman and Charles Moore stayed behind, not just for the good of their school, but also to treat their fellow classmates. Despite the disease being highly contagious, the boys survived and helped many of their classmates do the same. Two years later, Letterman and Moore decided to start a new fraternity that would forever carry on the maxim "the great joy of serving others."

Phi Kappa Psi came to the university in 1920 with its Oklahoma Alpha chapter. The chapter flourished, producing men such as Judge James D. Fellers (class of '32), who served as president of the American Bar Association, and astronaut Owen K. Garriott (class of '49).

Across the nation, however, Phi Kappa Psi would come into a period of struggle. In the 1980s and '90s, chapters of Phi Kappa Psi in Texas, Arizona and Ohio were closed due to hazing and alcohol abuse, often by the fraternity's national council, which feared an institution founded on service had lost its way. Phi Kappa Psi at OU had its own tragedies in those turbulent

The Phi Kappa Psi house.

decades. Over Christmas break in 1983, a fire broke out from the boiler that destroyed the house. While some students had left possessions there over the break, thankfully no one was injured.

Such was not the case on December 1, 1994. Early in the hours of Thursday morning, twenty-odd Phi Kaps gathered on the front lawn of their house to celebrate success on a fraternity ritual. The tradition at the house was to shake the flagpole—a crowd laying hands on it and shoving back and forth to create a wave motion up the three-story metal column. No one knew its clear history, whether as a collective challenge to unquestioned banners or a rejection of the 1920s flagpole-sitting fad. Whatever the origin, brothers had shaken the flagpole for years, and this was their time to show their spirit.

It wasn't the first time the fraternity had done it, but it would be the last. During the furious celebration, the pole broke just over the heads of those shaking it. The rest of the pole plummeted, swinging toward the ground and hitting Jason Henry Wittrock, a twenty-year-old sophomore in journalism, from Okarche. The pole caused a major injury, and he was pronounced dead at Norman Regional Hospital the next morning. True to the spirit of service at Phi Kappa Psi, his organs were donated.

The public stood aghast at another fraternity prank, but it was genuinely an accident. Investigation by the administration saw no account of hazing, and university police confirmed that alcohol had not been involved. Wittrock's sister Jayne Suess cleared those accused. "We aren't blaming the university; we're not blaming the fraternity. It was not their fault. If this had been a group of independents, it would just have been considered a freak accident."

Winter came on bleak as finals wrapped up and the boys went home for Christmas break. That spring, the house sat empty as the fraternity faced a temporary suspension after desecrating a teepee, meant as a prank without understanding of the significance of the Native American ceremony. The next fall, the brothers were back in the house. Something else seemed to have moved in as well.

The activity focused on the top floor. All through the night, brothers heard someone walking heavily from end to end and down the stairs. Late nights were nothing unusual for a boisterous frat house, but they were perturbed that whoever was stomping around wouldn't at least try to be quiet. As people began to discuss hearing the sound, some brothers admitted to being in the hall and hearing them even though no one else was around. Several brothers began sitting up to wait for the sound and then jumped into the hall to catch the stomper in the act. They found it empty.

Other strange events began plaguing the boys. Electronics mysteriously started themselves up without anyone touching them, and light switches turned on in the middle of the night. Things never seemed to be in the same place a brother had put them. It wasn't long before several brothers decided the house had become haunted, and they wondered whether it was Jason. He seemed upset, possibly perturbed at returning to an empty house that spring and summer, facing the afterlife alone until his brothers returned.

While some of the Phi Kappa Psis were convinced it was Jason, others denied that the house had a ghost at all. When a group of paranormal investigators were invited to come to the house, several brothers hid in the basement and made ghostly moaning sounds into the vents. Their voices were caught on the investigators' electronic voice phenomenon recordings, confusing the investigators before they discovered the culprits. The data was deemed unusable for research, and the investigators left without conclusive evidence one way or another.

The matter of the ghost became a divisive point at meetings and during informal talks. Many believed, many others didn't and a few felt that, even if the house were haunted, it was something that was best ignored. Letting the issue rest won out in the long run.

Officially, the house isn't haunted. Get a Phi Kap alumnus talking, though, and you may hear a scary story or two.

EVERLASTING ART

Jacobson House

Worlds collided at 609 Chautauqua Avenue to create a mix of Swedish, American, French and Native American that was truly unique. The man behind it all was Oscar Brousse Jacobson, born in 1882, in Westervik, Sweden. Like many of his fellow Swedes, he was part of a migration to the New World seeking new lives with new opportunity. At eight years old, his parents brought him to Lindsborg, Kansas, where a number of Swedish immigrants like him had settled. He was a daydreamer and a young artist, studying at Bethany College to earn his bachelor's in 1908. From there, he went on a grand tour of Europe, studying at the Louvre, in Denmark and in his homeland of Sweden. His studies brought him back to Yale in the United States and then to an unlikely new frontier: Oklahoma.

The Jacobson House.

The university in Norman had been rapidly expanding over its first three decades. In 1903, President Boyd brought on violinist Fredrick Holmberg as the first professor of fine arts. Holmberg quickly outpaced the position and became dean of a program that drew in more and more professors to grant students new opportunities. In 1915, he wanted to expand the program again, to add physical art to the school that had done so much with music, oratory and drama.

Holmberg hired Oscar Jacobson, who must have reminded him a little of himself. Both were Swedish immigrants raised in Kansas, both had studied at Bethany and both had aspirations that reached to the heavens. By 1924, Jacobson had become the head of a whole rank of professors in the School of Painting and Drawing, which became today's School of Art in 1929.

In addition to the school, Jacobson was tireless in his own improvement, returning to Bethany for a PhD in 1941. While on his adventures in Europe, he had met, wooed and married Jeanne d'Ucel, a Frenchwoman who was an artist in her own right. They decided to build a home of their own style as they settled in Norman, something that the town had never seen before.

It was a very wide home, built with front columns and enormous windows to let in natural light. At a glance, few Normanites thought much of it, but those who saw it up close were amazed. The columns continued inside the house to a huge main dining and living room. French doors led onto an enormous back porch, which became a stage for the backyard theater

The back porch served as a stage for private productions.

where Jeanne hosted home-written productions. Jacobson did much of the construction himself, not only out of artistic drive, but also necessity, with labor shortages in World War I. His hand-made scrollwork around the garage harkens back to Swedish design, and the huge southern enclosed porch is reminiscent of European salons.

The whole house was a gallery. Jacobson hung his own work of southwestern landscapes (he painted over six hundred in his career), as well as those that he collected on his travels. Music and laughter poured from the house as the professor and his wife hosted there for fifty years. Some of the most memorable events were the drum circles put on by Jacobson out of his love for Native American culture, which was best exemplified in his work with the Kiowa Five.

The 1920s brought on a renaissance among Native Americans. Through the nineteenth century, white settlers continuously poured into native lands, often moving them to reservations in events such as the Trail of Tears. Even under-populated reservations proved fixations for land-hungry eyes, such as the lands opened for later land runs in Oklahoma during the 1890s. The Native Americans, meanwhile, were encouraged to give up their previous ways and join the white culture. Buffalo were hunted to near extinction, and

Indians who had long depended on them were allotted farms for agriculture. At boarding schools across the country, Indian children were taught English and disciplined for using their native tongues.

Some, like Jacobson, were horrified at the devastation of so many cultures and fought to bring them back. Along with Professor Edith Mahier, he encouraged young Native Americans to explore their roots and bring new life to their traditions. Much of his focus settled on a handful of art students who came from the Kiowa reservation near Anadarko. Under his tutelage, they refined their drawing, painting, dancing and singing; with all of the resources he could muster, he found them fame. James Auchiah, Spencer Asah, Jack Hokeah, Stephen Mopope and Monroe Tsatoke collectively became known as the Kiowa Five. They were joined by Lois Bougetah Smoky, who combated not only the discrimination against Native Americans but also prejudice as a woman in the arts.

The dedication to native art was a far cry from what the Kiowa Five had seen growing up. Auchiah recalled being caught painting while in elementary school and, as punishment, forced to skip dinner and finish his art. The reprimand proved ineffective as the young Auchiah thought it was permission and excitedly called out, "I would rather paint than eat!"

Jacobson and the Kiowa Five.

Mopope had a much better experience when caught doodling in the sand: tribal elders quietly taught him to paint on canvas made from skins, in the Kiowa fashion. As they came to the University of Oklahoma, their talents were not only recognized but also celebrated.

While art was the core of their education, Jacobson found that dancing brought the most attention to the Kiowa. They dressed in traditional ceremonial garb and sang the songs of their people as audiences watched with wonder. He held many powwows at his own home, giving space for storytelling, as well as the songs and dances. As their popularity grew, benefactors allowed Jacobson to take the Five on tours. National tours turned into international ones with Jacobson's contacts in Europe, and the Kiowa Five became world celebrities before graduating and going their separate ways to endorse native art in all its forms.

Jacobson retired from the university in 1954, though he continued to use his home as an art gallery and gathering place for the arts for another decade. When he died in 1966, his house was bought as rental property before eventually being sold to the university as its campus expanded. It had come under disrepair, and some thought the best use of the land might be as a parking lot.

Fortunately, concerned Normanites raised new awareness about the house and its rich history. The Jacobson Foundation renovated the house and had it listed as a National Historical Site. There, it has established a new gallery of Native American art and hosts events it feels would make Jacobson proud. Many feel that Jacobson himself attends, even fifty years after his death.

The paranormal activity around the Jacobson House has continued for decades. As an old, hand-built house, it is filled with sounds of creaking floors, even with no one walking on them. The front door notoriously opens itself at night, despite being latched and locked. Former director Russ Tallchief chuckled as he remembered going to the house night after night to meet with police called by the alarm. "We decided it was the Jacobsons coming back to check on us."

Inside the house, things seem to reorganize themselves when no one is looking, but the most haunting are the voices.

Several years ago at a fundraiser, a student with the Native American Student Association was in the kitchen with a friend. A voice called out her name.

She turned to her workmate. "What?"

"What?" he asked in return.

"You said my name."

"No, I didn't," he said.

The voice called again, this time with his name.

The two felt a chill and hurried to finish up their work. Although the voice was surprising, she said it wasn't particularly frightening, just very strange.

One of the most memorable moments at the Jacobson house happened in the summer of 2014, as crews completed setting up for a masters show. It was a warm day, with only slight breezes to break up the muggy air. Everyone was drenched with sweat from lifting crates, unpacking them and carefully hanging paintings and arranging statues.

Just as they set up the final painting and began to catch their breaths, a huge blast of wind came through. Doors banged against their hinges. The whole house shuddered. Then the wind was gone.

Rather than feeling unnerved by the sudden gust, everyone had an uncanny sensation of calm, even cheerfulness. Chairman of the board of trustees Daniel Brackett said he had the feeling that "Jacobson was smiling," and the wind was his way of showing it.

The foundation is happy to have its house haunted by Jacobson, along with, many believe, his wife and many of their guests, including the Kiowa Five. They feel it keeps them on their toes to keep up a dedication to art that Jacobson himself carried to the grave and beyond.

IV
AROUND TOWN

Cleveland County began its organization as County 3 of the Unassigned Lands and was very nearly called Lincoln County before voters decided it would be named after Democratic president Grover Cleveland, who oversaw the opening of the territory. In the 1890 census after the land run, the population was 6,605; by 2010, it had exploded to over a quarter million. Each one of these people has a story, and many of those stories go on long after they are dead.

Some of the stories of Cleveland County go back to the time before white settlers came to the area. Legends speak of Indian burial grounds all over the region, and it is possible that there may be some in the thousands of unrecorded years of the land's history. Archaeological evidence is limited, although it is clear that the region was used for hunting. Where there were people, there must have been burials.

Sheryl Campbell, who says she has witnessed strange activity all her life, awoke one night with a ghost standing at the foot of her bed. He was tall, statuesque and dressed in ceremonial costume complete with a feathered headdress, an unusual sight for the apartments behind Heisman Square. He told her very seriously that the land on which she slept was a sacred burial ground. It was her duty to tell everyone in the complex about it so that they may respect the land.

"I really don't want to," Sheryl replied.

The Indian insisted. So, begrudgingly, the young woman walked from door to door telling everyone what the Indian had told her. She was

Cemetery for the Denver community, east of Norman.

mortified, but embarrassment seemed much preferable to the ire of a ghostly chief.

Joe Griffith relates that there are numerous unregistered cemeteries all over town; he himself has relatives resting in unmarked plots. An uncle told him that one could always tell an unmarked grave due to the appearance of cool moss rather than grass over the ground, often taking the shape of a rectangle over where the body rests.

One particular area rumored to be a burial ground is the Sooner Mall, particularly Dillard's. Clothes on the racks sometimes shiver as if someone unseen is looking through them. Objects on shelves reorganize themselves. In the women's changing area, the sounds of sobbing sometimes ring out. Customers have repeatedly stopped attendants to say they should check on the poor woman inside, even though all of the stalls are empty. In addition to the movement and sounds, another ghost appears as an elderly man sitting in the shoe section. Rookie salesmen have attempted to approach him several times, only to find that he has disappeared in the blink of an eye.

Even though we all have or know stories, Oklahomans are a down-to-earth lot who rarely spring into tales of ghostly encounters. When the topic does come up, however, we begin to share a little more of the stories we carry with us.

THE NORMAN BUBBLE

Oklahoma rests squarely in what is called "Tornado Alley," an area of North America where meteorological conditions routinely collide to churn out one of nature's deadliest forces. Cold, dry air descends from the Rockies in the northwest, while warm, dry air blows up from the southwestern deserts. Meanwhile, the warm, moist air of the Gulf of Mexico flows northward. These different fronts combine like water rushing through a sluice, becoming highly turbulent and forming eddies that spin out of control as tornadoes.

For the most part, Norman has been fortunately spared from nature's wrath. According to the National Oceanic and Atmospheric Administration's National Weather Service (fittingly located at the University of Oklahoma for its tumultuous weather), Norman's first measured tornado was in 1945 during September, a less often but not unheard of time of year for tornadic activity. Over the next decades, a few F0 or F1 tornadoes appeared, hardly noticeable inside the storms that accompanied them.

Downtown Norman in the 1940s. *Courtesy Cleveland County Historical Society.*

Locals often compared the weather with Moore, just eight miles to the north. In 1893, just a few years after the land run settled the community, two tornadoes struck on the evening of April 25, the second one killing thirty-one people. Additional tornadoes devastated the town in 1937 and 1973. On May 3, 1999, an especially destructive tornado, one of many that night, killed thirty-six people and injured nearly six hundred more. Lives were spared by an F4 on May 8, 2003, though two people were killed on May 10, 2010. Tragedy struck especially hard in 2013. On May 20, two dozen people were killed, many of them children at school, felled by collapsing debris or drowned while finding cover in flooding basements.

According to Rick Smith, warning coordination meteorologist in the Norman Forecast Office of the National Weather Service, there is no known reason why one town is hit especially hard and another seemingly spared. He notes that radar-based weather data only goes back to the 1950s. Anything before that is based on eyewitness accounts, and even those rarely go back past 1889. While it may seem that we have witnessed many tornado seasons, on a meteorological scale, all of our research is based on the blink of an eye. Smith admits, "We don't have enough data to make a solidly scientific judgment."

Where science has yet to deduce a cause, a host of old wives' tales attempt to give an answer. One of the most popular theories is that topology directs the path of the tornadoes toward the wide, low valley of Moore and away from the more hilly Norman area. Rick Smith agrees that topology does affect tornadoes, but the conditions that form them are thousands of feet up where the hot and cold air mixes. The low Oklahoma hills may have a miniscule impact on tornado directions, but anything short of mountains are negligible.

Another old wives' tale is that Norman is protected by a mystical bubble. Folks say that there is a sacred ancient Indian burial ground somewhere in town, with suggestions for its location ranging from Brookhaven to OU's campus to Hall Park. While all of these places have seen a good deal of construction, none of them have given up the telltale signs of archaeological evidence. Still, people have sworn for decades that there must be something magical about Norman to give it a shield against severe weather.

If there was a bubble, it must have popped in 2010. On May 10, Norman suffered two simultaneous EF4 tornadoes. One struck downtown, tearing up roofs and dumping torrents of chilly rain. Another went from the west of town, across Lake Thunderbird, over Little Axe and Pink. Three people were killed, and over eighty were injured.

Another tornado passed through the far eastern part of Norman in 2013. Lasting over fifty minutes, the tornado glided from the southwest, as they typically do, before turning almost ninety degrees and heading straight south. One television meteorologist famously noted, "In my entire life, I've never seen that."

Normanites, who had for so long carried folklore of invulnerability, sought explanation. Those who believed in the "Indian burial ground" explanation were determined to find out what could have been disturbed enough to cause an end to the perceived bubble. Fingers began to point to the 2006 destruction of Mount Williams.

Known as Mount Norman to outsiders who drove past it on I-35, the enormous earthen mound was leftover from a target range set up by the US Navy for pilot training in World War II. A town landlocked by more than four hundred miles seemed a strange location for a naval base, and cartoons of the time lampooned the decision. In truth, it was a very clever move, arrived at by happenstance.

In 1941, the University of Oklahoma Press's director, Savoie Lottinville, was traveling by train when he met Captain K.B. Salisbury of the U.S. Navy's Bureau of Aeronautics. The two began chatting, and Salisbury happened to ask if there were any interest in those days at OU in flying. Lottinville was proud to describe the brand-new airport that had been built by the university after a donation from the Neustadt family in honor of their uncle, World War I pilot Max Westheimer. Salisbury was impressed and asked, "Would you be willing to lend it to the navy for the duration of the war?"

Gears were set into motion, and soon the navy arrived in Norman. It rapidly expanded the airport to turn it into a training field to meet the needs of war effort, buying up land to the west and north. Dozens of buildings were put up, including hangars, barracks, a one-thousand-bed hospital, a swimming pool said to be the largest in the Southwest and an auditorium nicknamed the "Great Oak Hall." Over eighteen thousand servicemen and women went through the base's training, many of them WAVES (Women Accepted for Volunteer Emergency Service), who were taught metalsmithing in the Aviation Machinist Mate School. The base even boasted its own navy jazz band, the Gremlins and the Corsairs, which hosted weekly dances at the Great Oak Hall.

Most often, the pilots were seen in their yellow Stearman N2S-3 trainers, buzzing in the sky. As part of the construction, a target area had been built west of the base, including Bullet Mountain, a huge dirt mound more than fifty feet high and four hundred feet long that would later be better known as

Air traffic still goes through the Westheimer Airport on Robinson.

Mount Williams. Pilots would practice strafing and bombing runs, dumping phony bombs and shooting live ammunition into the dirt.

As the war drew to a close, the navy began cutting back. Training was among the first things to go, but the Norman city government and its chamber of commerce successfully lobbied the navy to keep the base open until 1956 to serve new recruits. Eventually, even it was closed, and Westheimer was brought back to its quieter days before the war. The hastily built dormitories were torn down, and the swimming pool was filled in, but Mount Williams remained standing over the city.

In 1982, bulldozers took part of the dirt pile for use in construction of a new hangar. Normanites were shocked and outraged. The university had spoken the year before of building a new runway and tearing down the old mound, but concerned citizens who thought of it as a civic landmark lambasted it with phone calls and letters. Finally, the university decided to sell the land to commercial developers and let them decide what to do with it.

Fittingly enough for a space once used as a World War II shooting range, it became the site of a Target department store. Many Normanites once again rose up and called for the salvation of the mound. A formal protest was planned on the day of the demolition, but construction crews were

A cartoon lampoons the idea of a naval base in Oklahoma. *Courtesy Cleveland County Historical Society.*

brought a day ahead of schedule to break down the earth. After years of seeing it as a milestone when arriving from the north on the interstate, it was gone overnight. Once the shopping centers began to open, however, the town's anger subsided.

All that remains of Mount Williams.

With Mount Williams gone, many Normanites feel we have lost the bubble. Believers in the topological explanation thought the sudden rise might destabilize eddies that could produce tornadoes, while others feel the hidden burial ground had its power broken. If it were a disturbed burial ground, no paranormal activity as of yet has been reported at the shopping center.

Whether the bubble will return, is gone forever or even existed at all will remain a mystery in folklore. As Rick Smith said, "There's just not enough data."

WALKERS ON THE ROAD

Northwest Norman

Roadways all over the world have famous stories of ghostly hitchhikers, filled with adventures of meeting someone decades after their deaths. An especially popular urban legend tells of a young man who saw a young lady standing on the side of the road in an old-fashioned dress. He offered her a lift home, and she accepted. The two chatted, really hitting it off. When they arrived at her parents' house, he turned to ask her out, but she was gone. Feeling determined, he got out, rang the doorbell and was greeted by an older man he assumed was her grandfather. When he asked about her, the old man became very grim. To the young man's shock, he explained that the girl was his daughter who died in a car crash on the way to a dance that very night ten years before (or twenty or thirty, depending on how the story goes).

Norman has its own cases of disappearing spirits on the road. One of the most perplexing is the farmer on Northwest Thirty-sixth Avenue before it becomes Telephone Road. The area is gradually developing as a popular thoroughfare to western Moore, with housing additions and a few offices and eateries. In times past, it was all long stretches of fields, interrupted only at the section line with a fence leading to the field on the other side.

Several independent eyewitnesses have spotted the farmer, and they have all described him as an elderly man dressed in heavy-duty trousers and a flannel shirt, topped with a dirty ball cap, a timeless style that could be from any decade of the past century. In all of the stories, he is simply walking down the road, and in all of the stories, he disappears without warning.

A worker for OG&E saw him and assumed he was one of any number of farmers checking the fields between the bank and the suburban houses. It was only when he blinked and the farmer was gone that he was surprised. The old man was by no means spry, and there wasn't anywhere for him to

The OG&E office on Telephone Road, where several eyewitnesses claim to have seen the old farmer.

have hidden. He even turned around to make sure the man hadn't fallen in the ditch alongside the road, but there was no sign of the farmer at all. When he arrived back at work at the OG&E station, he asked around about the strange event. Many fellow workers rolled their eyes, but just as many nodded and said that they had seen him, too.

People who have seen the old farmer like to believe that he once owned the land off Thirty-sixth Avenue. His connection with the land that he cared for is so strong that death itself cannot keep him from coming back to check on how the crops are doing. As houses and businesses continue to march over old farms, more traffic has come to the area, and more people claim to have seen him. Some take his presence as a warning to respect the land. They fear what might happen to him when urban sprawl finally consumes the land.

The farmer apparently isn't alone on the long, straight roads in the farmland northwest of town nicknamed "Ten Mile Flats." One evening, after her baby was born, Lara Kelly took the baby for a drive with her mother, Sally Austin. The gentle rocking of the car is often used as a trick to lull babies to sleep and give parents a little time alone with their thoughts.

Long roads in Ten Mile Flat are said to be the site of ghostly walkers.

Mother and grandmother had come along for the ride, and they soon met with other company.

A young woman, "not more than twenty," was walking on the north side of West Robinson between Thirty-sixth and Forty-eight Avenues. It was just becoming dark, with the sun setting over the Canadian River as it meandered under the boughs of the trees. They decided it was a little strange for a young woman to be out in the middle of nowhere at that time of night, so they pulled over and asked if they could take her somewhere.

The girl agreed and climbed into the car. She had "long, dark hair," and she wore a thin, short dress "like a nightgown or a burial shroud."

They talked with her a little, and the young woman said that she had just had an argument with her mother. She was fairly tightlipped, still clearly upset. When they had gone up the road a little farther, she pointed out a spot where she wanted to be dropped off.

It seemed even more secluded than where they picked her up. No houses were around, just the dense woods nearer the river. They stopped the car like she asked. After she got out, they drove away with uneasy feelings. After only a few yards, Lara decided she couldn't leave the girl there. They turned around, but the girl was gone.

Lover's Lane

Ten Mile Flats

For over forty years, the unsolved mystery of the brutal murder of two college students continues to plague Norman law enforcement.

On May 9, 1970, the Sigma Alpha Epsilon party was still in full swing at 11:30 p.m. It was Saturday, and the partygoers were young, with a great deal of energy to spare. Twenty-one-year-old David Sloan and his nineteen-year-old date, Sheryl Lynn Benham, decided to retire from the party for some alone time. They headed off in Sloan's 1966 Pontiac GTO and were not seen again until Monday morning.

They were found locked in the trunk, both dead. Their bodies were riddled with bullets, at least ten shots from a .22-caliber gun. Benham was stripped naked.

Shock flew through the small town. Lover's Lane was known by most people in town as a place for high school and college students to sneak away and park with their significant others. Northwest of town, it was a secluded stretch of Robinson Street that continued beyond Northwest Sixtieth Avenue. An overlooking hill in the east gives a tremendous view of the sprawling plains with dotted farmhouses. Going closer to the river, a secluded grove of trees offers not only a beautiful view of the Canadian below but also a sense of privacy.

Word of the strange murders sent the town into a frenzy looking for the killer. Evidence was scarce around the crime scene. Sloan's billfold was missing, but when officers investigated his earnings at a local restaurant where he worked, they ruled out robbery. He simply didn't have enough money worth killing over.

Fingerprints were taken from the scene. They proved clear enough to be used, and they were male but did not belong to Sloan. The Norman Police Department began searching through its "known police characters in the metropolitan area." Rumors began to spread that it wasn't a one-time event: this was just the first time for a would-be serial killer. He may have even attempted to strike earlier but been scared away. Parents became fearful, shotguns were kept loaded in houses and few dared to visit Lover's Lane again.

Chief Bill Henslee sent out a call for any tips on suspects, soon leading them to Ponca City. A vagrant laborer had been picked up hitchhiking on I-35 just a few miles from Lover's Lane. Officers arrested him, thoroughly questioned him, but were unable to link him in any way to the killing. A pair

A private road that once led to Lover's Lane.

of brothers had been found with blood-stained clothes in their Oklahoma City apartment, but rigorous questioning with polygraphs showed that it was animal slaughter, not human.

Some locals, like Mrs. Glenn Titus, were not surprised by the randomness of the murders. Living nearby the scene, she had a strange sense of calm about the murders, not fearful as if they had been "indiscriminate breaking-in or just shooting someone." Instead, she thought that the murder was intended, and Sloan and Benham were not just picked by chance.

Sloan's fraternity began a fund to pay a reward for any information, but the money went unclaimed. Police promised "complete confidence," hoping that anyone who might have been out in the grove that night, but afraid to admit their whereabouts on a moonlit evening, would come forward. Despite all of the community effort, the case never overcame its brick wall of lack of evidence and became cold.

A 1987 article reflecting on the murders noted this lack of evidence: "No witnesses, no footprints, no tire tracks." Even the little evidence of the fingerprints proved inconclusive. Police found a broken branch used to sweep up any prints, showing the murderer knew just what to do. It was a perfect time, too: Norman was crammed with out-of-town visitors to a demonstration on campus, a carnival downtown and numerous end-of-school parties.

A new chapter to the strange story opened in 1991 with the arrest of Frank Edward Gilley, a Norman police officer at the time of the killings who had resigned shortly thereafter. He was thirty-four at the time of the slayings, and rumors went around that Gilley had a history with Benham, but his attraction had been unrequited. Twenty-one years after the deaths of Sloan and Benham, testimonies varied. A farmer remembered the shots being at sunrise with two men standing over the car. Other witnesses were certain it had been Gilley. They said that he skulked around the area catching loiterers and abusing his police authority with threats. He was said to make them answer questions about their sexuality, and one woman said he requested she go into the woods and strip for him.

Two witnesses gave corroborating testimony about police involvement. Both, driving at different times by the curve that led down the road toward Lover's Lane, saw a police car, along with another car. One said she remembered seeing the trunk of the second car open. They both also said that they had given reports to the police but that they had never been contacted again. These reports were missing from official evidence, leading to accusations of police cover-up and conspiracy.

In February 1971, another double homicide rocked Norman. Policeman Bryan "Butch" Green was caught by James Roberson in an affair with his wife, Ronna. Roberson grabbed Green's service revolver and gunned them both down. Roberson was acquitted that September.

Green had been a friend of Gilley, but soon after his death, Gilley began to call out Green as a leading suspect in the Lover's Lane murders. As he was no longer on the force by that time, his accusations fell on deaf ears. Green's sister noted how agitated he was in the weeks leading up to his death, which she believed was orchestrated to keep him quiet.

In the new trial, strange evidence was brought forward. Retired Oklahoma Crime Bureau agent Ken Jacobson, who was instrumental in reopening the case, said that he had been approached by Green on November 24, 1970, months before his death. He told how Gilley had borrowed his white station wagon from time to time, the same car that witnesses had identified as being driven by him when harassing them at Lover's Lane. Gilley had told Green to lie if he were ever asked about Gilley's .22 rifle collection. Although the report was filed, nothing came of it.

Ultimately, Frank Edward Gilley was acquitted. The evidence was too sporadic to prove anything, and the drama of the conspiracies proved too much for the courts. Former police chief Bill Henslee was indifferent about the case and thought accusations of him being part of the conspiracy were ridiculous. "There's no one man that can do that. I'm just not smart enough."

The Lover's Lane Murders earned a short-lived spotlight in the national news, but their infamy has never left Norman. Some believe that the couple's spirits still haunt the woods. Initial stories came from the few daring teenagers who were willing to venture back into the tree line by the Canadian River and brave the possibility of an attack by a serial killer. No hook-handed figure or escaped inmate ever appeared, but they did believe they heard whispers, some angry, telling them to "Go away." Skeptics said it was just the wind, just like the sounds of scratching over the roof and trunk of their cars.

Soon the private road that ran down to the grove called Lover's Lane was gated with signs warning against trespassing. Attempts to contact the murdered couples were drawing the wrong sort of crowd, and locals were fed up with it. Today, a few foolhardy teens might try to get out there, but the path is difficult and may very well cause trespassers to end up inside of a jail cell for disturbing neighbors.

With Lover's Lane closed, high school students have found a new hangout at the Brookhaven Cemetery, said to be haunted by some of the many people buried there. Brookhaven is a peaceful graveyard with few readily attested stories of ghostly activity, but it serves as a spooky spot where couples are certainly willing to hold each other close. Those seeking greater thrills travel south of town to the abandoned meatpacking plant, where rumors tell much wilder stories of the paranormal.

I DARE YOU

Malone Meatpacking

Malone Products, Inc., was once a bastion of commerce on the south side of Norman. It began on the dairy farm of Paul and Rosa Malone in 1951. The couple was hardworking and diligent, reinvesting their profits whenever they had them. Eventually, they diversified with founding the Malone Chili Company, using beef from cows that were not-so-profitable with their milk. The buying and selling of meat for the chili turned into a whole business empire known as Malone Products. It was a family business, and the next generation expanded into New Mexico and Arkansas, becoming a significant institution across the South. Sonic, Kentucky Fried Chicken and Dairy Queen became routine partners.

The center of the empire was a meatpacking plant on Cedar Road, just east of Highway 77. A rusted wreck is all that remains of the building today, quickly falling apart from disuse and the elements. In its heyday, the building was a proud three-story facility with sheet metal walls covering an array of cranes that lifted the heavy beef carcasses slaughtered nearby. A few fences of the feedlot may be seen, but the trees that back up to the old building have swallowed up much of the land. It is a treacherous place, filled with hidden footfalls and easily broken steps, where anyone could fall and end up severely injured or worse.

According to legend, that is exactly what happened. A worker at the plant was caught off guard while standing on a platform. Some say that a swinging crane that had dropped its meaty payload struck him. Others suggest that he leaned against a railing that gave way or that he simply slipped on the spilled blood and bile from the dripping cow bodies. All of the stories agree that he fell to his death, his neck catching one of the lines and snapping before anyone could come to his rescue.

Another version of the story claims that the worker's death was no accident. Facing hardships—whether financial or romantic, depending on the teller of the story—the man decided to end his own life. While his co-workers loaded felled cattle onto conveyors and into grinders, he climbed to the highest platform, where the cranes connected to the beams of the ceiling. He wrapped one of the cables around his neck and jumped.

The legends of the supposed death are diverse and get better with time. If there were a hanging at the meatpacking plant, it was kept quiet either out of respect for the man or in an effort to keep bad publicity away from the business. Still, the rumors continue to fly, circulating especially among high schoolers looking for something exciting to do. In their stories, the man returns every night at midnight to reenact his horrendous death.

The fascination of seeing a ghost drives curious teens to the old plant in the wee hours of the night. There, outside of the lights of the city, they find their way over and through the debris, using the flashlight apps on their phones. Everyone has a story where a friend of a friend actually saw the ghost, but few claim to have seen it themselves. Several stories of adventures to the meatpacking plant end with friends hilariously abandoning them and driving back to town laughing, while the teller has to walk, akin to cow-tipping and snipe-hunting expeditions.

While it routinely serves as a destination for a bored summer night, the derelict meatpacking plant is legitimately dangerous. Police have chased several groups of teenagers out of there, not only for trespassing, but also to keep bodies away from sharp metal spikes and platforms liable to give way under any weight. If the building does not already have a ghost, it might very well some day from a kid trying to find evidence of the afterlife and ending up doing so the hard way.

NORMAN'S FIRST CEMETERY

Johnnie's Charcoal Broiler

It's an unassuming corner of Main Street that heads west toward I-35, an area well known for its restaurants. The whole street has its share of pizza places, taco places, chicken places and the more exotic Mediterranean or Asian cuisine, but not one of them is more down-home than the burger places. The corner of Main and Berry has hosted a number of burger joints, along with other businesses, but its first formal designation was as Norman's town cemetery.

Now commercialized, the corner of Main and Berry was once a burial ground.

The graveyard was established in 1889, shortly after the land run. Along with water and a postal service, it was a universal civic need. Older settlers and those who met their ends tragically young were buried simply, often in graveside services, since few churches had yet been erected. Many of them did not even receive markers, only plain wooden crosses that were most likely soon removed.

As the town grew with an explosion of population, however, it was clear that the land was needed more by the living than by the dead. By government order in 1890, the bodies were disinterred, and the graves were moved, reburied in new cemeteries established as the town gained its footing. Small communities outside of town absorbed some of the reburied bodies, such as the Denver Corner graveyard, started in 1891.

The corner soon developed. When I-35 was established in the 1950s, it became a significant thoroughfare in town between the new highway and downtown. Restaurants popped up to feed hungry motorists, such as Sooner Dairy Lunch, opened in 1954. Customers did not even have to get out of their cars; they simply pulled up and called in their orders in the height of atomic age fashion.

In 2004, the corner became home to a Johnnie's. The restaurant chain is named for Johnnie Haynes, a Californian who came to Oklahoma to continue his career in the food industry at the Sky Chefs in Will Rogers World Airport. He moved on to manage Oklahoma City's famous Split-T restaurant for eighteen years and then ventured out on his own with the first Johnnie's in 1971. The diner served to fill a nostalgic gap as carhops gave way to drive-thrus, but Haynes kept his drive-in stalls in addition to a drive-thru, as well as comfortable tables and booths inside. Tasty Americana food and multiple styles of delivery were a winning formula, and Johnnie's has since expanded throughout the metro area.

During the remodel to turn the corner of Berry and Main into Johnnie's, it was noted that it had once been a cemetery. Employees and patrons who had visited the previous establishments remembered that not all of the graves had been marked, so how could one possibly be sure that they had all been moved? Still, construction was completed, despite superstitious ideas of waking the resting dead. Mayor Harold Haralson commemorated the site with a plaque "to these pioneering souls," but it apparently did not placate the spirits.

It was soon evident to workers that something about the restaurant was not normal. Even before they knew about the first cemetery, strange things kept happening. Blenders, fryers and stoves would turn themselves on. Boxes

The 2006 commemorative plaque.

fell off shelves even when they were set back away from the edge. Workers had to go around constantly turning off a register that had suddenly started up or clean up a mess no one had made.

An older customer stopped by one time to mention the history of the plot, remembering back to the days when it was a gas station. Even then, he recalled, strange things happened. He then told them about the cemetery and cynically assured them, "They didn't move all those graves."

The most famous ghost appears as someone walking into the freezer. Descriptions of the ghost are vague, something people might see out of the corners of their eyes, but it's clearly a person. It walks through the kitchen a short way and then opens the freezer door to slip inside. Time and again, managers have gone in after what they assume is a customer who has gone past the Employees Only sign. Despite seeing someone enter and hearing the freezer door slam, no one is inside. Other times, people enter the freezer and sense someone there, like a glimmer that disappears when they try to look for it.

The ghost in the freezer isn't the only one present. Late one night, after all of the customers had cleared out, a few employees were closing. There was no rush, so they hung out at the counter chatting about this and that.

Suddenly, out of the empty seating area, a lady's voice called out, "Would you be quiet?"

The employees froze. Their eyes scanned the tables and booths. No one was there.

The voice returned to explain, "I'm trying to sleep."

Before it could say anything else, they rushed through closing and went home.

Theater Eight

Hollywood Cinema

After the installation of I-35, life in Norman moved away from the small-town ideals of independent, unique institutions. Visitors to town wanted brands they were familiar with, whether restaurants for dinner, hotels for sleeping or stores for shopping. Things needed to be bigger, faster and come with more options. Movie-going was no different; as the single-auditorium Sooner Theater with hand-painted royal shields closed down, the massive Hollywood Theaters opened up on the quickly developing western side of I-35.

What is now the Regal Spotlight Hollywood Theaters 14 began as a collection of ten theaters down the hallway from the cinema lobby, oddly ending with theaters eight and thirteen. The smell of hot buttered popcorn and the sound of booming state-of-the-art audio equipment filled the air for months as the first theater opened with its showing of *Titanic* in 1997. Over the next year, sales were promising enough to complete the western wing and add theaters nine, ten, eleven and twelve.

During the construction, a worker on the wall shared with theater eight had a lethal fall. The tragedy was an accident, new safety measures were taken and construction was completed. Soon, the projectors were rolling in four additional theaters filled up by Normanites eager for Hollywood entertainment.

A new tragedy struck theater eight when a man had a heart attack in the middle of a film. His family hurried to tell the usher, who called an ambulance. Theater staff worked to keep the man comfortable until paramedics arrived. He was taken to the hospital but sadly did not survive.

Both of these deaths are suggested to be the cause of the ghost that haunts theater eight in the Hollywood Cinema. Most of the haunting stories come

West of I-35, the theater was part of Norman's shift toward a new commercial center.

A spirit is said to meander in the hall near theater eight.

from the projection room at the rear of the theater. Employees have noted the room becoming strangely cold at times, despite the heat pouring off the bright lamps and machinery. They feel a presence there, standing and watching the film alongside them.

Some projectionists claim to have actually seen something shadowy in the room. They work in the other projection rooms and are familiar with the tricks of light coming from the films, but there is something altogether unnatural about the dark manifestations that stand and sometimes move toward them.

Equipment there is notorious for breaking down, but more perplexing are the times when problems prove to have no source at all. Rattling, rasping sounds are a common complaint among workers, who shut down the projector and find nothing amiss. The strange sound continues even when all of the equipment has been shut down. Several projectionists have quit after being haunted through the night by the rattling.

Outside of minor annoyances, the ghost in theater eight does not seem to cause much turmoil. Some say that they have seen a spectral man in the theater itself, and others say that he haunts the hallway up to the balcony game room. Whatever the case, it seems to have decided to spend its afterlife watching films, which is as good a fate as any.

THE CATACOMBS

Stubbeman Village

The student population at the University of Oklahoma fell from 6,935 in 1939 to 3,769 in 1945, almost halving class sizes, due to young men and women turning their attention to the war effort. When World War II ended, they were ready to return to classes, and the GI Bill ensured that more than ever could attend, free of charge. The university, which had largely been cutting back anything that didn't contribute directly to the school, was suddenly inundated with applications. OU hated to turn away anyone who was qualified, and so the school exploded with new teachers and students.

The problem became where to put them all. Temporarily, the university found space to expand in Campus Corner, the collection of shops, diners, laundries and boardinghouses to the north. Its first purchase was Albert Pike Hall on the corner of Boyd and University, the dormitory built by Masons from McAlester. The building was renamed Whitehand Hall, after Professor Robert Whitehand, who took a leave of absence to become Captain Whitehand of the Army Air Corps. He died fighting over France shortly before the war ended, and the university used his name to commemorate all of the soldiers who had given so much for their country. The dormitory was packed full with students, so many people coming and going that it was nicknamed the "Oklahoma Hotel." For married students, the university established row after row of tiny prefabricated houses that became known as Sooner City.

Over the next few years, OU caught up with the waves of new students. A south oval was established beyond the Bizzell Memorial Library, lined with new buildings for physics, education, geology and biology. Farther south, across Lindsey Street, huge new dormitories were built, including Cate Center for college coeds and the monumental Towers that housed hundreds of students each.

Just as Campus Corner had sprung up to meet the needs of students in the north, the expansion south brought about a row of shops that became known as Stubbeman Village. Through its long tenure serving students, the space

The old Cancer Corner.

included soda fountains, convenience stores, textbooks, Italian and Mexican eateries (like Pinocchio's, with never-ending breadsticks) and the infamous Mr. Bill's bar, where many students had their first beers, legal or otherwise. When OU began banning all tobacco from campus in 2012, everyone from the dorms who needed a cigarette walked across the street to congregate at Stubbeman, which earned the nickname "Cancer Corner."

One of the most famous spots in Stubbeman was the upstairs single-auditorium theater. It made for an excellent place to see cheap movies or get some alone time in the dark with a significant other, but rumors stated that it held more secrets, including a murder. The versions of the story differ greatly from a business rival to a hobo who was caught by malicious thrill-seeking students. Whatever the case, the upstairs earned its own nickname, the "Catacombs," because of the strange earthy smells. Others said the nickname came about from people finding the dried-up bodies of animals, practically mummified, again and again without explanation.

For many years, the second-floor theater was used by the Chi Alpha organization of Christians on campus. One former leader related the tale of being there alone one evening while painting scenery for a sketch. The room suddenly seemed to become cold, and then she felt she wasn't alone. Something began speaking, not intelligibly, but in a tortured moan. She immediately called friends for some company.

Cancer Corner came to an end when the university purchased the land and the tobacco policy extended to the shops as well. The Catacombs are used for storage now, earning the nickname from a shocking number of dead animals found there. While feral cats or a few pests might be expected to get stuck inside and starve, some people who work there believe there is something at work drawing them in and taking the life out of them.

HUNTERS

Dave Blue Trading Post

An old marker stands at the corner of Forty-eighth Street Southeast and Highway 9, pointing the way to what was once one of the first long-term settlements in what would become Norman: the Dave Blue Trading Post. Today, Cedar Lane runs haphazardly over isolated hills and down valleys covered with trees. Approximately 140 years ago, the land was equally

A historical sign pointing the way to the Blue Trading Post.

rugged, though treeless, and a man standing on top of the hill could see for twenty miles or more in any direction.

It was here that two Cherokee brothers, Dave and Jim Blue, set up shop. After the Civil War, as Jesse Chisholm began establishing his trading posts, the Blues did the same a little farther north than his post, in what is today Lexington, Oklahoma. The land was dry, but Dave Blue determined it was more important to have visibility than quick access to water in the creek that ran at the foot of the hill. By the time Abner Norman and his surveying crew arrived in 1873, the Blues had already built up three buildings, most likely a barn, store and house. Their survey also showed a six-acre cultivated field that had already taken in at least one harvest. When exactly they arrived was a mystery, as with much of their history.

By the time the Blues established their trading post, the Oklahoma cattle drives had begun to decline with westward shifts in the railroad network. Another shift in 1880 brought the rail line farther south to Caldwell, Kansas, which revived the Chisholm Trail for a time. Not much is known about what the Blues did before their post, but between the heydays of the cattle drives, the brothers were in the business of buffalo hunting.

Several interests combined to bring about the near-extinction of the buffalo from the Great Plains. Native Americans and whites alike hunted for valuable meat, which drove down any hope of returning to stable populations. On top of that, commercial hunting slaughtered millions more for hides and bones, which were ground into bone meal and fertilizer. Buffalo proved a hazard to the railroads, with their mile-long herds halting locomotives and causing tracks to deteriorate, so many offered a bounty simply for bringing in proof of a dead bison. Hunting became strictly about profit, and buffalo were killed in such numbers that meat was largely left to rot. Other plots against the buffalo were politically motivated, hoping to eliminate the Native Americans' food supply and encourage their dependence on the federal government and manufactures. Out of the estimated sixty million head of buffalo before the introduction of hunting on horseback and with rifles, fewer than eight hundred remained by 1890.

Dave Blue led whole teams, populated by Cherokee and Creek, on hunts through the region. In 1873 alone, they packed two wagons full of buffalo hides and hauled them to Atoka, which was then the nearest rail depot, at just over ninety miles from Norman, and famous for the nearby Battle of Middle Boggy Depot. While the Blues' reach went farther west, the last wild buffalo in Pottawatomie County was shot by Jesse Chisholm's son William, in 1876. Eventually, the herds were exhausted, and the Blues turned to different sources of income.

Legends around the region have long hinted that the Blues were cattle rustlers. Many Texas ranchers didn't want to use Chisholm's eastern route because it came too close to the fringe of civilization. More westerly routes were vacant of human life, making them safe from riffraff who could easily sneak a few heads out of the thousands that were being driven north. Supposedly, the Blues were among these rustlers and had used their earnings to set up a permanent post, although money soon began to run low as the cattle trails began to taper off. Nearby Pottawattamie and Chickasaw ranchers were highly suspicious of the brothers out on the lonely prairie.

Others thought of the Blue brothers as pioneers in an unsettled land. Their trading post brought a point of civilization to a rough land. This service to the origins of Oklahoma warranted their historical marker, as well as the naming of local waterways after them. Twin creeks leading to the Little River became Dave Blue in the west and Jim Blue in the east. Later, with the formation of Lake Thunderbird, these became coves continuing to bear the names of the rugged explorers.

While many people had different opinions about the brothers, a few had very dark concerns about their operation isolated in the middle of the prairie. Legends said that their outpost was built on top of a hill so that they could see anyone around for miles and know when they were truly alone. Sometimes single travelers would come along to ask for lodging or a few trade goods. If these travelers went missing, it was easy enough to believe that the wild prairie had swallowed them up, creating a perfect cover to kill them and loot the bodies. Supposedly, a whole collection of bodies was found in shallow graves outside the trading post after the Blues' own mysterious deaths.

There are differing reports on what exactly happened to the Blue brothers. Some state that they had traveled up to Cherokee territory, where they ended up in an altercation that turned violent. Others cite reports of a raid on the trading post, either by a posse led by federal marshals or a regiment of United States Cavalry.

The story goes that the posse was moving through the territory clearing outlaws from their hideouts. The Blues would have seen them coming from miles away. When the horsemen arrived, though, the Blues themselves were just getting back to the trading post. An argument of some kind arose, and the Blues fled. The posse followed and, according to legend, shot Dave Blue dead in the eastern creek and Jim Blue in the west. What exactly they had done remains a mystery, but some believe it was the discovery of the Blues' victims that prompted this action. Others believe it was a corrupt posse attempting to shake down the brothers.

Since their trading post was largely self-sufficient, the Blues had built up a good deal of profits from their buffalo hunting. Folklore says that they kept their fortune as gold and silver coins tucked into saddlebags, ready to be moved at a moment's notice. When they saw the posse coming, they hurried to Little River and hid the saddlebags under a rock outcropping. Upon their return, they showed they had no money. An argument arose, and hopelessly outgunned, the brothers fled.

They were chased to Little River, where Dave, the leader of the pair, was killed. Jim was taken on to lead them to the treasure. Some say that he gave up the hiding place and was then killed. More adventurous storytellers say that Jim refused to give up the location of their silver and gold, and it remains buried to this day.

Some sixty years later, the Oliphant family came upon a Colt percussion revolver in the field where East 120th would run today. It was the proper age and type for the frontier in the 1870s. Older siblings speculated that it

Spirits are said to rest under the waters of Lake Thunderbird.

was left by a member of Jim Blue's gang, dropped at half-cock, with three chambers already fired. If he had made a final stand against the posse, a little farther east of the creek that bears his name, it might very well have been his.

Another sixty years after that, vacationers at Lake Thunderbird came across a more chilling discovery: a human skull. Seven-year-old Jared Melton was swimming near Clear Bay on a warm July afternoon in 2006, when he stepped on something hard beneath the mud. Curious, he and his family dug it up and found a cracked human skull. They called police, who rushed to investigate after a pair of disembodied feet had been discovered two months before. This skull, however, proved to be much older, and its cracks were wounds from a heavy-caliber gunshot.

Across Lake Thunderbird from Clear Bay was, in fact, a rock outcropping, now sunk under the brown water. Most of it was cleared out in the 1930s, when a flood prompted Normanites to dig out a channel to contain the Little River. In the 1870s, it would have overlooked the river, a recognizable landmark with plenty of crags for hiding treasure. The river would have been as much as fifteen feet deep and twenty feet wide with steep banks on either side, a spot few would come to unless they had good reason, such as outlaw brothers on the run from a greedy posse.

The pasture near where the Blues once traded.

Today, the hill on which the Blue trading post once stood is now covered with trees, introduced after the turn of the past century, and a cellphone tower, from the turn of this one. During the 1889 run, the land was staked by U.N. Shelton, who turned it into the first cotton farm in town, and later became stables for private riding lessons. Where the Blues once hunted buffalo and ran from an armed posse in the Wild West, now youngsters have their first barrel races.

MONSTERS

Lake Thunderbird

Water is precious to life, especially in the rolling, dry Great Plains. The land that would become Norman has long been blessed with creeks flowing to the Little River and the larger South Canadian that watered buffalo herds and cattle on drives. Settlers after the land run supplemented their surface water with wells tapping Oklahoma's rich aquifer, but as the population of Cleveland County continued to grow, it was soon clear that the area needed something more: an artificial lake.

Lake Thunderbird is teeming with creatures of all kinds.

Ideas for damming the Little River and building a lake go back as far as 1936. The United States Bureau of Reclamation had built dams throughout the West to create reservoirs that would control floodwaters and allow for irrigation. Some of its most famous work was the Hoover Dam and the corresponding Lake Meade, completed in 1935. Norman wanted the same, but it wouldn't prove economically feasible until 1954. The Norman Project came into being in 1961, adding a larger reservoir to serve the growing Tinker Air Force Base and the southeast side of Oklahoma City, as Lake Stanley Draper was already too small.

In 1965, the Norman Project completed its mile-and-a-half-long dam. The soon-to-be-flooded land was bought up and reorganized, rerouting Highway 9 and moving several farmsteads out of the area. Rainwater began to accumulate in 1966, giving birth to the fledgling Lake Thunderbird. Over the years, it would grow to cover an area of more than five thousand acres and reach a depth of over sixty feet.

In the economic recovery of the 1980s, Oklahoma started to boom with oil production and high crop prices. Oklahomans invested their newfound wealth in recreational activity, and many of them turned to the new lake for entertainment with fishing, boating and swimming. Newspapers reported a surge in drowning deaths. Locals began to whisper that the lake had been built over an Indian burial ground.

Like much of the Norman area that supposedly hosts lost cemeteries, there is no way of telling what might have happened in the thousands of years before the land became settled. It may very well have served as a burial ground at one point or another, but it seems unlikely that settlers would bury their dead so close to their drinking water. Temporary sites like hunting camps may have done differently. Even so, there is no evidence beyond the wealth of arrowheads found throughout the area.

For several years, many refused to go to the lake for fear that spectral hands were reaching up through the water to grab victims and drag them under the rust-colored waves. Others suggested it was the spirits of Dave and Jim Blue, working to keep people away from their buried treasure. Skeptics pointed to the growing number of newcomers to the lake, saying that it was simply a statistical probably that so many people would lead to more accidents. To give their case credit, when the visitor population dropped off with the bust in the later '80s, the drownings also decreased.

When a rash of new drowning deaths occurred in the 2000s, a new culprit was targeted: the Oklahoma giant red octopus. Famous to cryptozologists, the octopus is believed to be the size of a horse and have leathery, red-brown skin. Its powerful tentacles reach up from the depths near the dam and pull down victims, whom it consumes nearly whole. Leftover bits would be eaten by smaller scavengers. Several people claimed to have seen flashes of red ropes or felt something like a tendril bump up against their feet and pointed to them as encounters with the creature. When a pair of disembodied feet was discovered in May 2006, still wearing jogging shoes, some people said that it was the remains of a woman who must have been grabbed off the land by the creature.

Thunderbird isn't the only lake to have rumors of the Oklahoma octopus. Lake Oolagah and Lake Tenkiller have their own stories, nearly identical to the sightings of ruddy red arms grabbing at swimmers. The similarity has caused some cryptozoologists to speculate that the octopus may be some kind of living fossil, remaining behind after the ancient shallow sea dried up. They point to Native American legends of a creature soft like a leech, but with tentacles around mouth instead of lips, that was said to haunt certain springs, all connected by a series of submerged caves. Perhaps the Oklahoma octopus was here all along, and we're only now noticing.

Problems arise with the scientific background of Oklahoma's lake creature. Firstly, all of the lakes are artificial and only a few decades old.

The seemingly quiet waters of Lake Thunderbird.

Even if the octopi were brought to the lake and discarded like the famous alligators of New York City's sewers, they are native saltwater creatures that would die in freshwater lakes in minutes. If it were a gradual progression of an invasive species, the octopi would somehow have had to navigate up rivers and cross several dams over ground to arrive at their mysterious destination. No evidence of the tentacle creature from Native American mythology has been seen in Oklahoma's springs, so it most likely remains a piece of legend.

Other people point to different river monsters, such as the mythical giant catfish. Like many fish, catfish grow as large as their environment will allow them, and people point to the fact that most of the drowning deaths happen in the deepest water of the lake near the dam. It is a notion that excites local fishermen.

An actual monster scare occurred in the 1980s, when people saw a creature swimming just beneath the surface. Alligators are not uncommon to the southeastern part of the state, and many feared that one might have swum up the rivers. More sightings of ripples in the cloudy water spurred near-panic. A massive hunt was called with park rangers in boats with nets and helicopters with spotlights. Eventually, the creature was caught. It was a family of beavers that had come out from the smaller creeks.

While people continue to whisper about a monster in the depths of Lake Thunderbird, others speak frankly about another familiar creature: Bigfoot. Shaggy, bipedal apes are most famous as Sasquatch in the Pacific Northwest and Yeti in the Himalayas, but they have also been spotted throughout the United States with the Fouke Monster in Boggy Creek, Arkansas, and the Skunk Ape in the Florida Everglades. The dense forests of southeastern Oklahoma, too, are said to be haunted by the Boggy Bottom Monster. Norman is no different, with its own Bigfoot wandering among the blackjack oaks in the state park and beyond.

The creature is always described along similar lines. It stands about seven feet tall, sometimes more, and has a long, shaggy coat of fur completely covering its body. A terrible smell accompanies the beast, and people claim to see its eyes flashing in the light. Although no one has ever claimed to have been attacked by it, something about the shy beast gives a sense of abject terror to anyone who sees it. Others are more curious, and researchers meet annually for the Cross Timbers Creatures Conference hosted at the Lake Thunderbird State Park by the Mid-America Bigfoot Research Center.

There are countless stories of people spotting something out in the trees, typically on the northwest side in the crook of the lake. The creature seems to stick to the forest, where it hides out among the branches. A man out chopping wood at his house near the lake suddenly caught a

A ranger station keeps watch on the tree line at Lake Thunderbird State Park.

glimpse of the creature standing waist-deep in the underbrush. A whiff of the terrible smell associated with the creature assaulted his nose. He dropped the wood and dashed into the house, where his wife noted that he was "white as a ghost." When he had calmed down, he was able to explain, "Bigfoot. I just saw Bigfoot."

One woman tells the tale that she and her sister were riding in the back of a pickup along Choctaw Road in the late evening. Her uncle suddenly slammed on the brakes, tossing them roughly, and her aunt and cousins sitting in the cab screamed. They looked up to see an enormous hairy creature walking on its hind legs near the road. After their panic (her cousin flailed so much he broke the windshield with his foot), the uncle recovered enough to speed away.

A fisherman down at the lake had another tale. He and a buddy were fishing late, when they began to notice the animals becoming quiet and moving away. It was evening, when they should have been most active, so the fishermen wondered what had spooked them. The quiet was broken with new sounds: loud, heavy breathing and branches snapping as something big walked over them. It ended with a splash into the lake. The friends decided whatever it was didn't like them being there, so they found another favorite fishing spot.

As far north and west as Moore, a pair of teenagers saw a creature under a bridge that may be related to Bigfoot. They described it as a "troll," obscenely ugly with a horrible stink and huge, despite being crouched down. It looked at them and grunted, and they fled into the night.

Researchers have found numerous unexplained footprints around the lake, making plaster molds of what look like ape tracks, too large to be real. Rangers at the park have not seen any glimpses of Bigfoot themselves and remain skeptical. It is clear that the area hosts bobcats, which may explain some of the sounds. Locals also say that jaguars still prowl in the trees, though most zoologists believe they were hunted out of the area decades ago. Perhaps there is more in the woods and water of Lake Thunderbird than we suspect.

Uncle Lew

Brendle Corner

One of the greatest criminal minds of the twentieth century lived much of his life just a few miles east of Norman. Llewelyn Morris Humphreys was born on March 20, 1899, in Chicago, Illinois, to Welsh immigrants. The family struggled in poverty, with only five of their ten children surviving to adulthood. They lived in a rented house in the Loop, a neighborhood packed with saloons, brothels and gambling houses circled by the elevated trains. Llewelyn quit school at age seven to make money for the family as a newsy, peddling papers. It wasn't long before the boy learned he could make much more money through intimidation, con art and theft.

Llewelyn was dragged before Judge Jack Murray at age thirteen, after being caught for larceny. The judge took a shine to the clever boy and hoped for more for him than a life of crime. He took the boy on part time as an assistant, tutoring him in law and politics. Llewelyn appreciated the judge so much that he changed his own name to Murray. The fatherly advising backfired, however, and young Murray only learned how to play the system better. When he was arrested at sixteen for a jewelry heist, he received only two months in prison. The prosecuting attorney, who was oddly lenient in the trial, touted a new diamond-encrusted wristwatch.

Murray's crimes rose to a new level with Prohibition and the sudden demand for alcohol. He hijacked a truck at gunpoint, but his daring was undone when the truck driver recognized him and afterward turned him in to his boss: Al Capone. Capone ordered his men to bring young Murray in for sentencing, perhaps with the lethal baseball bat that made Capone famous. After a few minutes with the brash young Murray, Capone decided Murray didn't need a lesson. Instead, he offered him a job as a driver himself.

For years, Murray diligently climbed up the criminal ladder. Whenever the heat came on after a job gone sour, he took off to visit his brother Henry, an electronics salesman in Little Axe, Oklahoma. Henry made a decent living from radios and phonographs, and he hired his brother as a salesman who rode out to call on local farmers. Lew Harris, as he called himself then, went door-to-door, which is how he met Mary Clementine Brendle. She was a witty, beautiful gal studying at the university, and Murray was smitten. They eloped to Dallas in 1921.

Clemie, as he called her, was well suited to Murray's lifestyle in Chicago. She taught him to blend in with the upper class with new manners, which brought a new air about him. He was still devious and ruthless at his core, but people saw him in a sudden cultured light that allowed him to become an adviser to the biggest gangsters in town. Al Capone was famously out of town for the St. Valentine's Day Massacre in 1929, which happened at the garage next to Murray's childhood home in the Loop, where he was visiting that day. Murray got out of the liquor business and went into managing

The house where Lew Harris met Mary Clementine Brendle.

labor unions, where his classiness truly paid off. His first conquest was the laundry industry, and he soon brought into the fold unions for bartenders, delivery drivers, garbage collectors and more. Clemie acted as the criminal outfit's secretary, using her impeccable memory to take notes in meetings where nothing was ever written down to avoid a paper trail.

Despite their carefulness, Murray was eventually caught for tax evasion after not listing $50,000 from his finder's fee for returning a kidnap victim as income. In 1934, shortly after the birth of his daughter Lewella, Murray went to prison for fifteen months. When he got out, Murray took his family to Oklahoma for a quieter life. Many speculated that Lewella wasn't actually his daughter, and he used the retirement as an excuse to get her away from prying eyes who speculated that she was the daughter of Clemie's unmarried sister and one of Murray's business partners—Capone himself.

The family settled in Brendle Corner, a tiny community off Highway 9. Murray bought up seven sections of land in others' names and built a charming native stone house. The home was outfitted with marble counters and fixtures, and shelves, cabinets, doors and trim were made from hand-carved pine and oak, much of the work done by Murray himself. As the popular "Uncle Lew," he hosted pool parties for neighborhood children and hired scores of housekeepers and groundskeepers from Little Axe. During the holidays, he personally loaded turkeys into his car and delivered them to less fortunate families; he also put on a Santa costume to deliver presents to children. Folks who asked about his money were told he was "in the laundry business."

Many locals still remember Uncle Lew and his generosity, but his position in the criminal world explained some of his quirky behavior. He insisted on purchasing the land around him to establish a compound complete with electronic alarms that were sometimes set off by hunters who were accidentally trespassing and suddenly caught and escorted away. The perimeter of the house had high cyclone fences and steel gates with padlocks and guards, as well as a lookout tower with twenty-four-hour surveillance. Thick rosebushes kept people on paths around the gardens. Rumors started that a whole series of tunnels ran through the property.

Murray maintained contacts throughout the criminal world. As convictions of tax evasion plagued his associates, accounts needed places to fake income, and Murray offered up his laundry business as a source, supposedly the origin of the term "money laundering." Murray also sought out opportunities for semi-legitimate investment, making campaign contributions to Nevada politicians who would legalize gambling and pass pro-union legislation. When Lewella graduated high school, Murray made some phone calls and got Frank Sinatra to take her to her graduation dance. Locals said he contributed greatly to the election of President Kennedy, although Murray "didn't like him much."

The law caught up with Murray in 1965, when he failed to appear for a court summons to testify. FBI agents spotted Murray at the Santa Fe railroad station in Norman, asking about train schedules to Mexico. He was taken to Chicago by U.S. marshals, where he joked to the grand jury, "Oh, I didn't know you were looking for me!" Murray posted $100,000 bail without blinking and went to his penthouse apartment.

A photo had been taken earlier of him reading a newspaper with his own indictment on the front page, so FBI agents decided to arrest him again on charges of lying to a grand jury in his joke. It was a strange action but legal enough. The agents were met at the door by Murray with a loaded revolver. He refused to recognize their warrant to search the apartment, and soon a fight broke out. Agents subdued the elderly man and confiscated thousands of dollars in cash, as well as a coded journal that has never been deciphered. They claimed to have left Murray in the apartment unharmed, but when his brother came to visit, Murray was dead and the apartment was torn apart.

The crypt of gangster Murray Humphreys.

Murray's ashes were taken by his former wife, Clemie, and his daughter back to Brendle Corner and laid to rest in a blue marble crypt. Their ashes joined him there, and the land was broken up for sale. Jay and Shandi Williams bought the two-story stone house, turning much of the former compound into paintball fields. They say that there has been no evidence of a haunting in the house, but others suspect that Murray's ghost still walks the property.

The ghost is said to be searching something out, walking, as if lost, from tree to tree. Local legend says that Murray left an emergency stockpile of cash, gold and jewelry buried on the land. He never had a chance to dig it up before fleeing to Mexico, so now this spirit seeks it out.

The spirit may also be someone made to "disappear" while visiting Brendle Corner. Many of Murray's Chicago associates came to visit him, and out in the country, nobody would have known if someone had left in one piece. Butch Smallwood, who now owns part of the property, said he routinely ploughed up old car parts as if entire vehicles had been dismantled and buried. He also relates the tale of a contractor doing some bulldozing work who ran across a rectangular sinkhole about six feet long and two feet wide.

"What do you think that is?" he asked.

Smallwood joked, "It's shaped just like a coffin."

The contractor announced he was done, packed up and left.

CRYBABY BRIDGE

Southeast 134th and Air Depot

One of the most popular urban myths is the story of the Crybaby Bridge. The stories come in many forms, from infanticide to accidents, but they all share the trope of a young child who perishes falling from a bridge. There is something mystical about the underside of the bridge and the trickling water below. It seems anything might be hidden in the depths and the shadows, and many believe the children whose lives end there leave something of themselves behind to cry out in the dark of night.

Just a mile east of Sooner Road on Southeast 134th Street, Air Depot's southern run from Midwest City is interrupted by a broken bridge. The

Half overgrown, Crybaby Bridge still stands.

story of its collapse is that a mother was driving over it one night, during a storm, many of the versions say. The bridge gave way under the car's weight, and both mother and child died in the horrible crash. The wreck wasn't discovered until days later, when police happened by on patrol. After festering in the creek bed, the sight was a horror to behold.

Since its demise, the bridge has never been repaired. Lost travelers may stumble upon it from time to time, but usually the only people to come to the bridge are those curious to hear the wails of a long-lost child. According to legend, those who stand on or near the bridge at night will hear the cries of the baby. For a long while, nothing will happen, but then a sharp sound will rise over the rustling branches and trickling water. The cries come softly at first and grow louder and louder until the listener can't stand the sound any more.

It is a story similar to others, but the local Crybaby Bridge is unique because it has a historical Crybaby Lake nearby. In an earlier legend, dating back decades before the other, a couple was in a small boat at a pond not too far from where the bridge is now. They were to spend a lovely day fishing, with their baby resting in the gently rocking boat, but something went awfully wrong. The boat capsized, tossing the young family into the murky water. The couple managed to save themselves, but the baby was lost in the weeds of the shallow pond. They searched frantically, but by the time they found their baby, it had drowned, wrapped in the tangles of mud and grass. Similarly to the bridge later on, locals said that they could still hear the gurgling cries of the child in the night.

While Crybaby Lake is one of a kind, Cleveland County isn't alone in Oklahoma with its Crybaby Bridge. Near Kellyville, a story tells of a woman with her baby driving fervently to escape an abusive husband. Her car careened out of control on the bridge, and while the mother and car were recovered, the baby was never found. Visitors supposedly hear the cries at midnight, and a few claim to see an unexplainable blue light.

McAlester has another tale of lost children, more sinister, with legends of repeated incest and the resulting children being thrown from the bridge to cover up their existence. The sounds of crying ring up from under the bridge at night. Legend goes further to tell of a ghostly woman wandering atop the bridge and over the rocks of the creek below, wordlessly searching out the murdered babies.

Other stories of crybaby bridges come from all over the world, as well as in the United States, in Maryland, South Carolina, Texas, Ohio and more. The prevalence of crybaby bridges has caused an uproar among folklorists, feeling

Gaping holes show where the bridge collapsed.

that many of them are contrived tales, purposely spun to make up stories that unfortunately may elbow out actual local stories of interest. Another take on the trope discusses it as part of the human condition. Waterways have long been seen as a method of cleansing or a gateway, perhaps to a realm where children who were robbed of their lives still go on as shadows.

THE BACK ROOM

Kendall's Restaurant

As land runs and then lotteries settled the western part of what would become Oklahoma, transport to the railroads became all the more important. While nearby Norman prospered due to its cheap city lots, the town of Noble became a major commercial center for young Cleveland County as the only place to have a bridge across the Canadian River. All of the farmers west of

Noble's impressive bridge over the Canadian River.

the river who wanted to bring their produce to market came through Noble, as did all of the manufactured goods delivered to the farms. The age of prosperity ended in tragedy when the bridge was destroyed in the Flood of 1904. A fire destroyed half of downtown in 1905 and another ravaged the other half in 1906.

It was a bleak time, but the town of Noble bounced back with a new downtown and a trained volunteer fire department to defend it. At the corner of Chestnut and Main Streets, a new brick building was constructed in 1909 by C.M. Hobaugh, who had bought the land from '89er Thomas Standifer. John Henry Stufflebean bought the building and turned it into Stufflebean's Grocery Store, which would continue in business for nearly sixty years. It was a prominent corner, as Chestnut had once led to the bridge over the Canadian. A livery stable stood west of the new building and would eventually be joined to it, creating a hallway out of the former alley between them. Across the street, the Cottage Inn Hotel once stood alongside the bank building, which has been there since 1902.

Today, the building houses Kendall's Restaurant, famed for its chicken-fried steaks and, increasingly, its many ghosts. Owners Dee Downer and Kim Lock first noticed strange activity when Kendall, Dee's daughter and the restaurant's namesake, didn't like going to the back room, which had a small play area for children. She told them, "The woman in black yells at me."

Staff soon began experiencing their own problems. After closing for the night, the last staff member is to sign out, close the kitchen door in the hall and turn out the lights. One waitress recalls doing all that, and as soon as

Once a grocery, Kendall's Restaurant serves customers in a building over one hundred years old.

she walked away, the door burst open and the lights flipped on. Others have had similar experiences. Joe, the cook, once tried to close the door and found it stuck against thin air. "It was like someone was playing a trick on me, pushing from the other side."

Customers, meanwhile, had different experiences. In the back room, a family was sitting with their little girl, who kept looking up at the play area and waving. Her parents asked who she was waving to.

"The little girl in the corner," she explained. No one was there.

Why the back room is so haunted remains a tantalizing mystery. According to Stufflebean's grand-nephew, the store once sold coffins out of the back. It seemed a strange thing for a grocery store to do, but census records show that one of Stufflebean's sons started a mortuary service in Paul's Valley, and it stands to reason he had a branch office behind his father's store.

With all of the activity, Kendall's has hosted several paranormal investigations, many directed by the Oklahoma Paranormal Research and Investigations (OKPRI) team led by Christy Clark. Using electronic equipment, the OKPRI team has captured several clips of the same woman's

The restaurant stands in what was once two buildings before the alley was walled in.

voice and a child's voice calling for "mommy." A motion sensor on the doors to the playroom went off so often that the team had to shut it off.

In Clark's psychic impressions, later researched by team historian Kathryn Wickham, at least five ghosts seem to walk the hall and the back rooms that once stood behind the grocery store itself. One seems to be a former worker for the livery stable, another a banker who committed suicide and another a butcher whom Clark felt was named Henry. The name spurred a hunt for butcher Henry Witt, who once killed his brother and escaped jail, but it became clear from family photographs of the Stufflebeans that they often went by their middle names. Kendall's Henry may very well be the original grocer back to watch his shop.

The "imaginary friend," a young girl in the play area, is another popular ghost, but none is as notorious or active as the woman in black. Her name seems to be Margaret, and local legend says that she committed suicide by

A booth where a paranormal investigator felt something brush her shoulder.

eating white oleander leaves. In sessions, paranormal investigators sit in the booths around the play area and speak with her, attempting to get her to reply to their questions by turning a flashlight on and off. It is a standard,

The playroom where children have a shared "imaginary friend."

though somewhat sensitive, flashlight set on a table without any natural reason to change.

During a recorded event, an investigator felt something brush past her. The investigator asked, "Margaret, was that you?"

The flashlight flickered and turned off.

"Can you turn it back on?"

It turned on.

Over and over, in answer to their questions, with no sense of rhythm that could be explained through electronics, the flashlight flickered on and off.

While Margaret has at times been troublesome, trying to bump plates out of waitresses' hands, perhaps in jealousy, and Henry might be trying to keep what was once the backdoor to his store open, the ghosts are welcomed in the restaurant. Dee says most of the activity is "lots of little things you don't think twice about." The bigger things, meanwhile, bring something unique to Kendall's. Where else can kids go to play with a little girl ghost?

Unquiet Halls

Griffin Memorial Mental Hospital

Like many places, Oklahoma has long struggled with the needs of the mentally ill in our population. When the territory began, there was little choice other than to send them east to somewhere they could be helped. The destination was Oak Lawn Retreat, in Jacksonville, Illinois. The cost was tremendous: $300 per patient per year, with $150 expenses for each person committed. Oklahomans felt they could do better taking care of their own, but a bill for a sanitarium in Chandler failed in 1895. Finally, legislators determined that a new Oklahoma sanitarium company could work on the campus of the former High Gate College, at the east end of Main Street in Norman.

Methodists established High Gate College as an alternative to public schooling. Rather than restricting education to graduate level, students were offered courses in grammar school and high school. Their first year in 1890 had 150 students; OU's in 1892 had 57. High Gate opened its first building in 1893, but fundraising was increasingly difficult for a school that openly advertised that students "desiring to have a good time will not find this institution to their liking," banned students from "places of amusement,"

High Gate Hall. *Courtesy Cleveland County Historical Society.*

and censored student letters. Eventually, it became clear that the community could not support two colleges. As OU outpaced High Gate, Boyd and High Gate's president, A.J. Worley, suggested combining the two. Instead, High Gate would be closed and its building turned over to become the new territorial sanitarium.

High Gate was remodeled and, on July 27, fifty-three patients came to Norman from Oak Lawn Retreat. Forty more arrived three months later when new security measures had been put in place. After offering a treatment plan for private patients suffering liquor and opium addiction, the population swelled so much that the sanitarium had to turn newcomers away. In 1898, the funding for patients was dropped to $200 each, and the company began to struggle with profits, eventually ending up in receivership. The next year, Dr. David W. Griffin was hired to run it while the courts sorted out the matter.

Griffin was horrified by what he saw when he arrived at the hospital. Previous focus had been on finances, which had left the care of patients in a deplorable state. New respect was given to treatment, and Griffin successfully appealed to the legislature to create a state institution in 1915. He even fought to change the name from Central State Hospital for the Insane to the more respectable Central State Hospital. It would later be renamed in his honor.

The hall becomes Oklahoma Sanitarium Company. *Courtesy Cleveland County Historical Society.*

Griffin focused on making life stable at the hospital. By 1930, he had turned the financial disaster into a self-sufficient farm. In addition to having a vineyard, orchard and acres of gardens, the hospital raised chickens, hogs and cows. The grounds had its own power plant, ice plant and laundry, with much of the work being contributed by the patients themselves. When Griffin retired in 1950, the hospital served some three thousand patients without cost to the state.

It was not without its struggles. In the early hours of April 13, 1918, a fire broke out in a linen closet in the men's ward. Steam whistles screamed into the night calling for help. Although many of the patients were evacuated, forty perished in the flames, the highest death toll of any fire in state history. One of the forty was claimed by his family, but the other thirty-nine were burned beyond recognition. They were buried together in an unmarked grave and known simply as the "unfortunates." Over the years, the grave was lost. It was only recently rediscovered by new scanning technology, and administration at the hospital determined to finally give them a marker.

Most Normanites immediately think of Griffin Memorial as the most haunted site in Norman. There are many strange and puzzling stories from the hospital grounds and many of the buildings, which are no longer used as the institution has cut back over the years. Poltergeists, unseen forces moving objects and making sounds, are the most common culprits, yet there are even stranger sights. One man told the story of going with a patient into

Veteran's Hall stands closed yet is still one of Norman's most beautiful and iconic buildings.

the courtyard for a stroll. A huge light, seemingly in the shape of an owl, suddenly flew from the blocked-off windows of the boarded-up Veteran's Hall, swooped over them and sailed back up into the night. They hurried back inside.

While Veteran's Hall is perhaps the most recognizable, with its arching roof and windowless walls, Hope Hall is said to be the most haunted. It is closed now, but many still remember strange stories from working there after patients had been moved out and it was converted to offices. Much of the old equipment remains, as much for decoration as for the lack of outside storage, serving as a constant reminder of the history of the building. It seems more than just the physical has stayed. A man came into work early one morning to find a woman in the office. She wore a long smock, the same outfit that patients wore long ago, and did not seem to notice him at all. Instead, she stood over one of the old machines as if she were working with it, checking dials and adjusting knobs. After a moment, she disappeared and has not been seen since.

Hope Hall.

A woman working in Hope Hall also had a story of coming in early. She was gathering equipment to go to other units to draw lab work on patients. While in the back part of the office, she looked up to see a black smoky figure just twenty feet away, by the bookshelf. The figure floated, not walked, across the room and passed through the double-locked doors. It then continued on down the hall and out of view. It was a long while before she told anyone about her experience, explaining, "I didn't want people to think I was crazy."

Building Nineteen is also closed up, though it is still used for medical records and storage. Two people there were sitting at desks, working calmly. Without warning, a pen jumped up from a desktop and flew across the room, narrowly missing a man standing nearby.

Another worker recalled walking through the third floor on night shift. He was retrieving medical records for admissions, something he had done many times, although it was a little spookier since he knew he was the only person in the building. Someone began whispering to him from just over his shoulder. He moved, and the voice followed him, closer to his ear. He got out of the building as quickly as he could.

One of Hope Hall's entrances. Wheelchairs rest on the caged balcony.

The Edsel Ford House.

The Edsel Ford House, named for the director of social work who passed away suddenly while at his desk in 1989, was once one of many houses that stood along East Main Street for doctors and administrators on the hospital's campus. Staff still use it today for fun meetings like retirement parties and overnight stays near the hospital, such as a string of winters in the early 2000s when there were debilitating ice storms. Many who stayed in the house told co-workers that they would never set foot in it again.

Something was in the house, seemingly living in it as if it the house belonged to it. All through the night, even though everyone was in bed, footsteps would walk up and down the stairs and around on the second floor. After lamps had been switched off, something came back to turn them on. People in the house constantly had a creepy feeling that they were being watched. Yet the ghost hardly seems malicious. According to his family, Edsel had quite a sense of humor and probably would have laid claim to being that ghost.

Rose Rocks

Noble

Oklahoma offers a strange geological formation unlike anywhere else in the world: the barite rose, or rose rock. It became the official state rock in 1968, after collector clubs petitioned the government with thousands eager to see the rock gain credit where it was due. No town holds rose rocks dearer than Noble, the "Rose Rock Capital of the World," where an annual festival brings music and pageantry centered on the rock.

Rose rocks form in a unique set of circumstances, found in a band stretching from Guthrie to Paul's Valley. It was once the shore of the inland sea, which, as it dried up, concentrated the barium sulfate. The barite formed crystals that grow out in jutting, rectangular shapes that intersect around a common core. All around the barite crystals, sandstone settled to hide the roses within the rock. As the sandstone wears away more readily than the barite in wind and rain, the roses "blossom."

While there are other forms of rose rocks, none have the same vividness as the red rose rock. Sharp aragonite roses, sometimes nicknamed "Indian money," are found in western Oklahoma as translucent crystals. Gray selenite roses can be found in the American Southwest, Mexico, Morocco and

Noble's water tower shows the pride of the town.

Jordan, which lack the rich iron deposits of Oklahoma soil. The vivacious red makes the Oklahoma rose rock unique in the world.

According to legend, the red came from the great tragedy of the Trail of Tears. Gold was discovered in Georgia in 1828, prompting white settlers to push into native Cherokee land. The altercations between the groups grew worse and worse, culminating in the Indian Removal Act. The Cherokee nation was sent westward to what would become Indian Territory, and as much as a fourth of the population died on the thousand-mile journey.

Many rocks are crimson, said to be colored with the spilled blood of innocents.

When they arrived in Oklahoma, the blood of the braves and the tears of the maidens dropped to the ground, coming to rest, along with the people who had survived. The stone blossomed in the form of the Cherokee rose flower, and that is why rose rocks can be found only in Oklahoma.

SELECTED BIBLIOGRAPHY

BOOKS

Butler, Ken. *More Oklahoma Renegades*. Gretna, LA: Pelican Publishing, 2007.

Rhyne, Jennings J. *Social and Community Problems of Oklahoma*. Guthrie, OK: Co-operative Publishing, 1929.

Schrems, Sue, and Vernon Maddux. *Norman: 1889–1949*. Charleston, SC: Arcadia Publishing, 2013.

Stine, Joseph G., and Nancy A. Stine. *The Rose Rock of Oklahoma*. Noble, OK: Timberlake Press, 1993.

Womack, John. *Norman—An Early History, 1820–1900*. Norman, OK, 1976.

ARTICLES

Associated Press. "OU Flower Child Slain in Mexico." *Oklahoman*, August 9, 1984.

———. "Second Foot Discovered at Lake Thunderbird Campground Near Norman." May 11, 2006.

———. "Skull Found in Lake Thunderbird Reportedly Very Old." July 25, 2006.

Cannon, Jane Glenn. "Long, Lost Grave of 'the Unfortunates' Discovered in Norman Cemetery." *Oklahoman*, May 12, 2014.

Cleveland County (OK) Enterprise. "RS Davis for County Treasurer." March 23, 1916.

Clifton, Zane. "1970 Murderer Left Few Clues in Pair's Death." *Oklahoman*, August 31, 1987.

Courage, Katherine Harmon. "Could an Octopus Really Be Terrorizing Oklahoma's Lakes?" *Scientific American*, December 19, 2013.

Donovan, Kevin. "Norman Loses 35-Year Tradition with Closing of Denco's." *Oklahoman*, November 24, 1981.

Hatch, Katherine. "All Looks Peaceful Killer Haunts Flat." *Oklahoman*, May 21, 1970.

———. "Fingerprints Checked for Clues to Slayings." *Oklahoman*, May 16, 1970.

———. "Probers Hunt Witnesses to 2 Killings." *Oklahoman*, May 15, 1970.

———. "Slaying Probers Ask Public Help." *Oklahoman*, June 3, 1970.

Killackey, Jim, and Robert Medley. "Victim's Family Lays No Blame in Fatal OU Flagpole Incident." *Oklahoman*, December 3, 1994.

McCormick, Meghan. "Hale Ready to Retire." *Norman (OK) Transcript*, May 31, 2008.

Minty, Chip. "Gilley Forgives Those Pursuing Him in Slayings." *Oklahoman*, November 13, 1991.

———. "Jury Selection Begins in 'Lover's Lane' Case." *Oklahoman*, October 21, 1991.

———. "'71 Death Adds Twist to Gilley Case." *Oklahoman*, October 31, 1991.

———. "Two Tie Police Car to Site of Murders Lover's Lane Scene Described." *Oklahoman*, October 25, 1991.

Norman (OK) Transcript. "Local News." April 17, 1896.

Oklahoman. "Darlin' Recipe Revealed." March 23, 1982.

———. "Dozers Bite Norman Mount's Dirt." October 14, 1982.

———. "Police Hit Brick Wall in Slayings." May 31, 1970.

Rieger, Hannah. "The Prince of Crime." http://ndepth.newsok.com/murray-humphreys.

Stafford, Jim. "Florida Firm Buys Food Distributor." *Oklahoman*, November 8, 1994.

United Press International. "Nudity Advocate Stuns White House." *Palm Beach (FL) Post*, November 4, 1973.

WEBSITES

Jacobson House. https://jacobsonhouse.org.

Johnnie's Charcoal Broiler. http://johnniesburgers.com.

Moore, Oklahoma Tornadoes (1875-Present). http://www.srh.noaa.gov/oun/?n=tornadodata-city-ok-moore.

Norman, Oklahoma Tornadoes (1875-Present). http://www.srh.noaa.gov/oun/?n=tornadodata-city-ok-norman.

OKRPI. http://www.okpri.com/Kendalls.htm.

ABOUT THE AUTHOR

Jeff Provine teaches courses on composition, mythology and the history of comic books. His writing career began as he pursued his master of professional writing degree at the University of Oklahoma with the *Celestial Voyages* series of historical steampunk novels. He blogs about alternate history, draws *The Academy* webcomic and recently published a young adult science fiction novel, *Dawn on the Infinity*. After creating the OU Ghost Tour charity walk, he wrote *Campus Ghosts of Norman, Oklahoma*, collecting its stories. He believes in ghosts, though he has never seen one himself.

www.jeffprovine.com

Visit us at
www.historypress.net
....
This title is also available as an e-book